Determination, perseverance, diligence. These are just a few of the words that come to mind when I think about James Richardson. Overcoming disastrous events in his life, continuing to deal with physical, mental and emotional residual issues, James meets challenges with a positive attitude and a thousand watt smile!

— Shelley Coull, Physical Therapist

Great Read. I couldn't put it down until I finished reading it. It brought tears to my eyes and a few laughs.

—Glenda Blake

Standing on Two Feet

To Eleanor – I hope you enjoy

9-21-2010

Standing
on
Two Feet

James D. Richardson

James Richardson

TATE PUBLISHING & Enterprises

Published by Tate Publishing & Enterprises, LLC
127 E. Trade Center Terrace | Mustang, Oklahoma 73064 USA
1.888.361.9473 | www.tatepublishing.com

Tate Publishing is committed to excellence in the publishing industry. The company reflects the philosophy established by the founders, based on Psalm 68:11,
"The Lord gave the word and great was the company of those who published it."

Published in the United States of America

ISBN: 978-1-61663-481-0
1. Biography & Autobiography, Personal Memoirs
2. Biography & Autobiography, General
10.05.21

Dedication

I owe a debt of gratitude to so many people who made this book a reality. I would like to thank all of my doctors, who have worked with me and continue to work with me on all my health-related matters. I really am indebted to my prosthesist, John Paul Donovan, who has tirelessly worked on my prosthesis to ensure that it fits well and works the way it is supposed to work. Without John Paul, I am convinced that I would be confined to a wheelchair for the rest of my life. He also introduced me to my physical therapists, Shelley Coull and Laura Morgan, who instilled faith in my brain and body. They made me believe that my leg wouldn't let me down; through therapy, they convinced me to trust it.

In order for me to trust my artificial leg, I relied on the aforementioned people, my parents, and on God. My parents worked diligently with me on all my physical therapy exercises—my gait and form. Whenever I wanted to give up, or whenever I said, "That's good enough. I am walking the best I can," my Mom and Dad refused to accept it, and they continued to push me to get better.

Thank you so much, Mom and Dad, for everything you have done and continue to do for me. Where would I be without my parents? I shudder when I even begin to think about it. I would probably be stuck in Florida as a ward of the state. Without my parents, I would have had no place to go. I couldn't return to the nursing home, my wife wouldn't let me come back home, and I had no leg. My constant and consistent faith in Jesus Christ as my Lord and Savior sustains me every day. It is so true, though I don't know who first said it: "You have a friend in Jesus."

I hope that this book is an inspiration to all our returning veterans who have unfortunately lost a limb overseas. Keep the faith, and trust in your doctors and your therapists, and you will once again stand on two feet and walk.

I would also like to thank all my editors at Tate Publishing for all their advice and encouragement through this process. I formally dedicate this book to my sons: Camden James and Bowdoin John Richardson. Not a day has gone by since my accident October 12, 2003, that I have not been thinking of you, loving you, and praying for you.

Table of Contents

Foreword

Clad in his typical LL Bean attire and equipped with a roll of toilet paper at his desk, Mr. Richardson was hands down my favorite teacher in high school. Richardson had a unique teaching style that facilitated knowledge in such a way that was ideal for my understanding and comprehension - a mixture of open discussion, lively debate and, most of all, humor. I remember Mr. Richardson would call on his students by their last names - shouting it as if he were summoning us from some great slumber at our desks to provide the correct answer for our family name's sake. It still cracks me up when I think of his Maine accent shouting the name, Mr. "Maaarrrtin!"

Richardson taught world history - a subject I honestly wasn't particularly interested in at first. None-the-less seventh period (my last class of the day) became a daily escape from the pimpled brace-faced repression that was sophomore year. It didn't really matter what kind of horrible day I was having - I knew Mr. Richardson's flannel-thick accent and hilarious classroom antics would bring comic relief to the day.

I remember seeing Richardson around campus before taking his world history class. It was hard not to notice him trudging the hallways with his prosthetic leg which he boldly and purposefully displayed in shorts (even in cold weather! Although he would undoubtedly argue that there is no such thing as cold weather in Tampa - but I digress). My first year of high school was the year he had returned from his accident. Like most freshmen I was nervous and desperately trying to find my voice. Seeing Richardson walk with such fortitude inspired me a great deal, and when I eventually took his class my second year I was able to find my voice through class participation. I gained a sense of confidence in my words and abilities that have served me well these six years I have known Richardson.

I am honored to be a part of his book. Putting a lifetime of thoughts and experiences into words is an epic task to undertake and for that I respect the dedication Richardson put into the creation of this book. For all he has done for me and all other comrades who had him as a professor I wish all the best to my favorite teacher, and my friend.

—Annemarie Boland

Preface

Who am I? And what am I looking for? What is my purpose in life? These are questions that have plagued me my entire life. Perhaps they have baffled you, too. Obviously, I know my name. It is James, but who is James? I guess I will begin by telling you everything that I know about James. I am a forty-three-year-old old male, but what is age? It is nothing but a number. You are only as old as you feel. Sometimes I feel like a teenager, and sometimes I feel like a retiree. I am a high school teacher—a successful one.

More on that later, but one reason for my success is that I relate well to adolescents. I still remember what it is like to be a teenager. Whether it is jargon, recreational activities, or even music, I attempt to keep abreast of the current phenomena and am rewarded in the classroom.

On the other hand, I often feel quite ancient. The music I listen to is now called classic. It is one thing to have a classic automobile, but it is another thing to be referred to pejoratively as a classic. I now like to nap. Old people like to nap a lot. Am I now considered an old person? I currently work in a large supermarket as a cashier—depressing I know—and I have to card people. Many of the people I card were born the year I graduated from high school, or even after I graduated. Once again, this is depressing. People say, "You are only as old as you feel," but at times, this does make me feel old.

My parents, with whom I live, are in their early seventies. Sorry, Mom—she is sixty-nine, but will be seventy once this is written. I can honestly say I would be nowhere without my parents. Who makes you who you are? Or what you are? Many people will argue that you, yourself, are responsible for what and who you are. I vehemently disagree. Many people maintain that life is a journey, and to a certain extent, I agree. We are all on a journey that we call life. What inspires our journeys to be different are the proverbial forks in the road that we all must take. Whether we turn left, bear right, get on the rotary, turn around—enough of this MapQuest metaphor. You get the idea. The ultimate goal of any journey is to get there. So what is the goal of the journey called life, which everyone is on?

The American Dream

Just about everyone would agree that the main goals of life are to be happy and have success. Here is where the road gets muddy, for as travelers, we often cannot agree on what constitutes success or happiness. For most people living in the United States, this equates to material wealth—possessions and money. This is unfortunate! Many people will do anything to get more, and often this means betraying others. People sacrifice their morals, their principles, and often their families to get ahead. I wish that I knew why. Many people defend this by saying they are living the American dream. What is the American dream?

As a student of history, I always thought that the American dream meant possessing the opportunity to do better than the previous generation. I was the first Richardson to attend and graduate from college. This obviously made my parents and family proud. I grew up in a home with two parents—a rarity today—and I have a younger sister. My family lived in an affluent town, which was a curse for my sister and me.

My father worked in a manufacturing plant for over forty years. He began working there when he was eighteen. He never graduated from high school; I think this bothered him. He married my mother, and they bought this house in 1961 for $11,000. My parents put their children before everything else. Isn't that what you're supposed to do when you decide to have a family? I firmly believe so.

The prosperous town where we grew up was Yarmouth, Maine. This was a nuisance for my sister Julie and me. We had an arduous time keeping up with the Joneses, who had all the nice clothes, cool toys, and took all the extravagant vacations. We never fit into this bourgeois community. It wasn't a lack of support from my parents. My father worked in a blue collar job in a baked bean factory. He got a second job in a distribution center when I was eight or nine years old, and he worked eighty hours a week.

My mother then became mother and father to us; we only saw Daddy on weekends. Mom did everything for us: checked our homework, carted us where we had to go, and helped us when we needed assistance. My father attempted to make up for lost time with us on the weekends. He bought snowmobiles and a dirt bike for me, which I rode when I was five years old. I would often go snowmobiling with my father into the wee hours of the morning. It was a blast.

My father practiced baseball with me on the weekends and vol-unteered as an assistant coach for my Babe Ruth baseball team. This helped me develop skills, and it helped him make up for lost time with me. My mother was my biggest fan. I can still hear her scream-ing in the stands for me to do well. Thanks, Mom and Dad.

I started varsity as a freshman for my high school baseball team. At that time, my American dream was to play professional baseball for the Boston Red Sox. I was a good player, but with age, my skills and my desire to play diminished. So what became of my American dream?

I realized early on that I would not play professional baseball. Growing up in a lower middle class home in an affluent community, my sister and I didn't have too many friends in Yarmouth. I got a job at Shaw's Supermarket as a freshman. My social life basically mirrored my employment at the grocery store. I made friends there. The people who worked there had to work there to have spending money. I was unlike most of my Yarmouth peers, who had every-thing handed to them on a silver platter. They didn't need spending money. I worked hard and saved my money to purchase a vehicle. I bought my cars, unlike my Yarmouth friends, who had their vehicles handed down to them or bought for them.

Buying a car gave me some freedom and independence. I started dating a few girls who worked with me. I dated a few girls, but I fell in love with, Candace Susan Henry. She was three years older than me. She was in college, and I was a sophomore in high school. Part of the American dream is being in love. I then decided to graduate high school early. Why? Did I do it because I loathed Yarmouth High School, or—more accurately—my pretentious phony class-mates at Yarmouth? Or, did I graduate early to be closer to Candy? Was it a mistake? I don't know. I graduated high school in three years. I am sure my class ranking suffered from this decision. I was in the top ten with my original class, but graduating early caused me to slip below the top ten. I decided to go to a local college—the same college my girlfriend attended, the University of Southern Maine, or USM.

I went there for numerous reasons. It was affordable. I could pay for it myself, so I didn't have to be a financial burden to my parents. This was important to me; I had seen my parents struggle to keep up with the Joneses on my sister's and my behalf. My father quit his second job, and my mother went to a two-year college and gradu-ated to work in Maine's largest hospital, Maine Medical Center, as a unit secretary. I saw my parents struggle financially and listened to their advice. I opted to major in accounting at USM. I had always done well in math, and I continued to do so in college, but I really didn't enjoy it, so I switched majors.

I always loved history, so I decided to study something I liked. This decision didn't sit well with my parents, who argued, "What are you going to do?" I didn't have an answer for this. I thought about writing the next great historical novel. I thought about teaching, and I remembered some of my teachers who had inspired me. I had one history teacher in high school with a speech impediment, and I really enjoyed his class; it was fun.

What made history class fun? The answer to that question shaped my educational future. Mr. Soule gave his students a voice in his class. They could argue and defend their points of view, even if they were unpopular. This dialogue was engaging, and Mr. Soule incorporated humor into the classroom discussions, which made class lively and enjoyable for me. I looked into what it would take to become a teacher. I learned that I would have to obtain a degree in education.

While I was attempting to figure out what I was going to do, Candy—a French major—was in her last year of college and about to go to France for a semester of studies. This was a traumatic time for us. We broke up for reasons that are unclear to me now. I wanted her to experience Europe with a spirit of freedom and not miss me too much. I argued that we could always get back together when she returned. In retrospect, this was a colossal mistake! I don't know why I thought that we should break up while she was in France. Maybe this was the adult thing to do, because I thought this was a once in a lifetime opportunity for Candy to experience life on a different continent, and I didn't want to hold her back.

Upon her return we got back together, but I wouldn't let go of what happened in France. To make a long story short, she *did* decide to live life to the fullest, but I couldn't seem to get over that. In retrospect, I was the one who was not acting like an adult. This is a mistake that still haunts me to this day.

Candy and I stayed together for a few months upon her return from France. She applied to and was accepted to graduate school for library science, and I took her to Rhode Island, where she attended URI. I had to think of myself first—something of a rarity for me. Where was I going to go to school? I didn't want to stay at USM, because I would have had to go to school much longer to obtain a degree in secondary education. I was a sophomore, and I wanted to graduate from college on time, so I looked at opportunities through the University of Maine system. The university system is a conglomerate of seven colleges within the university framework. I looked at all of them, USM being the first. I considered strongly the flagship of the University of Maine system, Orono, because I had some friends there, but the financial requirements were too cumbersome. I opted for UMPI, the University of Maine-Presque Isle. I resigned from Shaw's and moved five hours away to UMPI. As a junior, I lived on campus, and I made two friends who were brothers, Mike and Jeff Soule.

We had fun together, and after a year, we decided to get a place off campus. We got an apartment and got involved in intramurals.

We dubbed ourselves SMAF—"I Smell a Farta"—as a pseudo fraternity, and we won many intramural events against many frat boys, including floor hockey. I graduated *cum laude* with a 3.5 GPA.

I got summer job at Crescent Beach State Park as a ranger; it was a great summer job. I didn't have to work very hard, and the fringe benefits for that job were excellent. Maine has a bottle law, whereby all cans and bottles are returnable for five cents, and many park patrons just threw their beverage containers away. As a park ranger, my job was to keep the park safe and clean. I cleaned picnic sites, mowed the lawn, and patrolled looking for park violations. I made two friends there—Paul Hodgedon and Glenn Tulloch. We are still friends to this day. Part of our job was to empty the trash into a dump truck, and take it to the dump. Before going to the dump, I jumped into the truck to pick through the trash to collect the returnable bottles.

Picking bottles and cans out of a cornucopia of debris—clam and lobster shells covered in liquid dubbed by Glenn as "mystery juice," not to mention kids' diapers—was a messy job...no pun intended. We saved the money and had park parties, where we drank copious amounts of alcohol. Our boss, John Scott, who we called "Big Guy," sanctioned these park get-togethers. I dated numerous girls who worked there as lifeguards.

At UMPI, I contemplated what was my hurry in getting out of school? I took the GRE exam for graduate school admission, and I applied to numerous schools, including Cornell. I was accepted to Marquette, where I received a tuition scholarship and a teaching assistantship. After going to an interview at Cornell on my motorcycle, I decided to attend Marquette.

It was a long trip—from Maine to western New York—to take on a motorcycle. This sojourn occurred before the days of Map-Quest, and many people—notably my parents—were against me riding a motorcycle solo across such a vast expanse. For me, this trip characterized the American dream: man versus the environment. I conquered the environmental conditions on my 1982 Honda, but my interviewer at Cornell was not impressed with my helmet and leather jacket. I guess I wasn't Ivy League material.

Fallona, a lifeguard at Crescent Beach State Park had just graduated from high school when we started dating at the park, and after that summer, she went off to Goucher College in Maryland. I was on my way to graduate school at Marquette University in Milwaukee, Wisconsin. I thoroughly loved our time together. I flew to see her in Baltimore, and she came to visit me in Milwaukee. After that year, we once again worked at the park over the summer and had a great time together. She returned to Goucher, and I looked for a teaching position. I was offered a position at a middle school, and I did well there. Karen and I stayed together, and I visited her as much as I could. On one visit, she gave me an Irish wedding ring, and I acted like a complete ass—I didn't recognize the symbolism and meaning of this gesture. For this, I am sorry. We broke up that year, and my life suffered. I was not asked to return to the middle school teaching position. I was out of a job, and to make matters worse, I had just moved out of my parents' house for the first time.

I was living in Portland, Maine, with one of my friends from the park, Glenn Tulloch. For the next year, I worked at L.L. Bean and collected unemployment. I didn't like not having a teaching job, but "unenjoyment"—that's what I called it—was not that bad, because I thoroughly enjoyed fishing. I brought brook trout back to the apartment for tasty meals; I was basically on a state-sponsored fishing team. I loved fishing, and instead of just bait fishing, I became a polished fly fisherman. To be a successful fly fisherman, I had to become one with the fish. It is a Zen-like experience, and for me, fishing became an integral component of my American dream.

What is the American dream? This is truly a conundrum, but I thoroughly believe that it is to be happy, to have a purpose, to grow, and to do better than the previous generation. In order to attempt to pursue this, one must have a solid foundation.

People get their fundamentals from their parents. I never really attended a church growing up, but I did receive a firm moral foundation from my parents. I knew right from wrong, because it was expected of me as I grew up, and I was praised for doing what was right. I never wanted to disappoint my parents by doing something wrong. I was aware of the struggles they endured to bring us up in that bourgeois town, and I refused to give them something else to worry about.

As a kid, I experimented with various things — namely drinking and recreational drugs — but unlike the majority of my peers, I never let them control of me, because I wanted so much more. I wanted to play baseball and do well in school, to make my parents — and, for that matter, myself — proud, and I realized this early, before my other activities hindered that. Though pride can be considered a sin, I consider it an integral component of the American dream. People need to have a sense of pride in their accomplishments. After giving the Almighty his due, personal pride is beneficial in that you want to continue to have a sense of achievement. I obtained a one-year sabbatical teaching position at York Middle School, and I dated a colleague from Auburn Middle School, Rhonda Baillergon.

I really wasn't proud of this, because I was personally and professionally treading water. I broke up with Rhonda, and I finished my assignment at York Middle School and looked for another teaching position. I went back to work for L.L. Bean and obtained many fishing supplies, which pleased me. In terms of the American dream, fishing was the only thing that consistently gave me pleasure, and life needs to be enjoyable — part of the aforementioned dream. I finally obtained a teaching position at Woolwich Central School, where I taught seventh and eighth grade social studies classes. I started dating a girl named Sheila, and things went well for a while. In fact, I moved out of my apartment with Glenn, and Sheila and I decided to move in together. I had many doubts about this decision, because there was someone else I couldn't get out of my mind.

Karen Ann was still in my thoughts, so I reached out to her and decided to end my relationship with Sheila. I moved to Dresden, where I found an apartment on the Kennebec River, which was a half an hour away from Augusta — the town in which Karen grew up. Karen had just completed graduate school at Boston University, and I hoped she would move back to Maine to be with me. I desperately wanted that to happen—to grasp that component of the American dream, which was turning into a nightmare for me. I had a relatively large lump on my right testicle, which had to be removed, because the doctor feared that it might be cancer. My sister, Julie, came from Boston to help my mother and me.

I went home to Yarmouth to be with my family after the operation, but a lot happened at the homestead, unbeknownst to my mother and me. My father was having a lengthy affair. He was living at home—having his cake, and eating it too. He didn't even bring me home from the hospital. Paul MacDonald, a friend of my parents, brought me home. The good news was that it was not cancer. I decided that living in Dresden was not for me, so I talked with a friend from my park days, Paul Hodgedon, and we decided to find an apartment and live together.

We found a decent place in the Deering area of Portland. We had fun and fished as often as we could. We branched out in pursuit of the elusive brook trout and salmon. Instead of just following the local Department of Inland Fisheries and Wildlife stocking list, we explored other areas that proved productive—Rangeley, and the west branch of the Penobscot River area. I loved fishing both areas, and I introduced Paul and Glenn to both areas. I bought a fourteen-foot Starcraft boat with a fifteen-horsepower Mercury motor. I had previously fished Rangeley Lake on this boat, and Paul and I later fished Rangeley in the spring and fall and did exceptionally well for salmon.

My principal at Woolwich Central School, Mike Macguire, and I talked about fishing, and he told me about the west branch area, so I decided to give it a try. I did really well and caught numerous fish, so I told Paul, and we had a great time catching a plethora of brookies and a few salmon. I bought a canoe and an electric trolling motor, and we loaded my Toyota truck with all the essential camping and fishing gear and took off. The area we fished was adjacent to Mt. Katadhin, and it was breathtaking. It truly is God's country. We fished from the canoe on the west branch of the Penobscot, and we worked numerous adjacent brooks and streams.

To work a stream is to read it and walk through it to find and catch fish. The tricky part is reading the brook. To read a river, you must be aware of the current and see the eddies; you have to notice the insects and attempt to match the hatch. Once done, you have to tie on a fly that resembles the hatch. This is called matching the hatch. If successful, you will fool the fish into accepting your fly as a bug, and it will rise and take your fly. Presto!—you catch the elusive trout or salmon. You look for pools where fish are congregating. Being able to do this is an essential element of the American dream for me. I would often work streams and brooks for hours at a time; catching fish is quite often easier said than done.

If a fish accepts the fly or bait and is hooked, the art of catching the fish has just begun. You need to play the fish in order to tier it out so you can land it. After it is landed, you have to decide whether or not to keep it. Fishing is a lot like dating in these respects. You have to attract the opposite sex, like the proper fly, and you have to present yourself to her; then, you must hook and play the fish. I think this is called courting.

I met a girl, Barbara Skelton, and we hit it off exceptionally well. At that time, I was approaching the American dream. I had a job I enjoyed, and I was good at it. I was falling in love with a girl, opening up to her and sharing all of my personality. I took her on my boat, and I occasionally brought her fishing with me. She was a waitress at a restaurant located on the water, and I visited her there on my boat. Things were going well.

Barbara spent time with me at the apartment I shared with Paul, and in my mind, I was contemplating the next step. I decided to ask Barb to marry me, and I did it by taking her fishing. I was fly-fishing an inlet or outlet of Sebago Lake, and I asked her to reach into my fly vest to get me my fly box. Lo and behold—she found a box ... not my fly box, but a ring box. I went down on one knee and asked her to marry me. She said yes! The fight was on.

We decided to live together, so I moved out of my apartment in Portland, and we moved to a less desirable neighborhood in South Portland. It was in the Redbank area, and—unbeknownst to me—my father's mistress also lived in that area. My work commute to Woolwich was taxing; Barbara and I talked about moving closer to my teaching job in Woolwich, but she wasn't in favor of that, because she said it would be difficult to find a good job as a waitress. I bought that argument—hook, line, and sinker. I explored other teaching opportunities, and I accepted a position in Bar Harbor. It was with mixed feelings that I left Woolwich Central School; I had been there three years, and I was liked and respected professionally and personally. As it turned out, this was a colossal mistake.

Barbara and I couldn't afford to live in Bar Harbor, so we found a house to rent in Southwest Harbor, Maine, which is located on the other side of Mount Desert Island. It was a nice, quaint place, with a view of the ocean. Barb got me a cat for my birthday, which I named Rangeley. This was very nice of her, and on the surface, things appeared fine. However, storm clouds were building off the coast and were threatening to come ashore. My teaching job was an eighth grade position, for which I was to teach social studies classes. This is what I believed when I accepted the position and resigned from Woolwich Central School to move.

When I arrived to teach, I was told that I would also be teaching English and math classes, which I was not certified to teach. I didn't let the powers that be know this; I assumed that they knew this when they hired me. I guess what they say about assuming is true, because I definitely believe that the administrative people at Connors-Emerson School were asses; I think that they felt likewise about me. They wanted me to become certified to teach additional subjects. If I had known about that, I would have never left Woolwich. I told them that they had hired me illegally to teach classes I was not certified to teach. People in power hate to be questioned, especially when they are culpable. That was not the only thunderhead rising.

Barbara initially worked at a restaurant in Southwest Harbor, but then she decided to take a job in Bar Harbor. At the time, it didn't really seem like a big deal to me. We had always worked different hours but made time to do things together during our time off. This became more and more rare. As a teacher, I worked a set schedule, but her schedule varied depending on the business's schedule. Increasingly, she was rarely at home, and I should have seen the writing on the wall, but I didn't. Bar Harbor is a seasonal place, where the population and business explodes in the summer, so why did Barb have to work more and more during the winter months? I should have known, but it still surprised me when Barbara told me that she was leaving me. Why did this happen?

We had always enjoyed each other's company and had fun together. We liked Acadia National Park and the surrounding ponds, hiking trails, and carriage road. We loved to spend time on Cadillac Mountain. I think that she wanted to do things after working her shift in Bar Harbor, but as a teacher, I was unable to spend time carousing and drinking; I had to get up early the next morning to teach. Initially, we did these things together when our schedules corresponded, but as time went on, we did less and less together, and she came home from work later and later. I found out that she was leaving me from Glenn, who called me at Southwest Harbor. Barb answered the phone and told him that she was leaving me.

She moved out and returned her engagement ring. I canceled all our joint accounts and looked for a place to live that I could afford. I found a cheap apartment over a garage and moved in. I cleared out the house in Southwest Harbor and loaded everything into my truck and boat and brought it back to my parents' house in Yarmouth. The apartment I rented over the garage was partially furnished, and Rangeley and I lived there for a couple of months. I decided that MDI was not the place for me. What had happened to the American dream? It seemed more like a nightmare to me.

Married

I resigned from my teaching position at the Connors-Emerson School in Bar Harbor and moved back to Yarmouth. A lot had changed at my parents' home. My father was having an affair. Once my beloved mother found out about these shameless acts, my father moved out to rent in Gray. She found out about his affair in the summer of 1995, and my father moved out of the house in August. My mother and I became even closer than we already were. We often went out to breakfast and dinner together. We relied on each other to overcome this tumultuous time for both of us. I looked for another teaching position in vain, and I worked seasonal jobs at L.L. Bean. I explored an opportunity to teach in other countries, and I was offered a position to teach in Cali, Colombia. I went to Boston with Paul to sign the papers and obtain a passport.

It was June 1997, and I was set to leave the United States in September. I applied for a teaching position at Madawaska High School, located some seven hours away, in the northernmost tip of Maine. I applied for this position because of what I learned about Colombia. I went to an interview and evidently did pretty well, because they offered me a position teaching advanced placement American history. I had never taught high school classes or students before; all my experience was at the middle school level. I had a decision to make. What was I going to do?

I researched Colombia and discovered that there was extreme social and political unrest rampant there. The seeds of these disturbances were fertilized by leftist guerrillas. The illegal drug trade was extensive in Colombia. After learning this, I opted to accept the teaching position in the St. John River Valley. I found an apartment and was set to move to Madawaska. Before leaving for Aroostook County, Paul and I went out to have a few beers on the shores of

Sebago Lake. While there, I met Lucinda, and we got along well. I moved to Madawaska, but I kept in contact with Lucinda, and she drove over seven hours to come see me. I thought that we had fallen in love. Was this actually happening?

A little history on this budding relationship seems necessary here. The night we met, I got lucky ... or so I thought. After sleeping together, I got her number, and in a few days, I called her. During the conversation, I asked her, "What would have happened if I didn't call?"

Lucinda replied with, "They always call." This should have told me something, but at the time, I was thinking with my other head.

Lucinda was a nurse who lived in Lewiston and worked at Central Maine Medical Center. She was divorced and had a daughter, Cassandra, who lived with her. Her ex-husband, Arthur Philbrook, lived in Auburn. I enjoyed spending time with Lucinda. She came to see me in Madawaska, and I would do the same to see her in Lewiston. Rarely a week or two would go by without us seeing each other. I believed everything that she told me. Lucinda said that she had been married once, and that she went to the University of Alabama for her nursing degree. One out of two isn't that bad, but I didn't learn the truth for years. Lucinda never really told me what went wrong with her marriage to Arthur. She just said that she never loved him.

In truth, she was engaged to a friend of Arthur's while at Alabama, but he died in a drunk-driving accident. Shortly thereafter, she married Arthur. This should have sent off some warning bells, but I was falling in love, and I guess it is true that love is blind.

Lucinda and I had fun together, and we were in constant contact via phone when we were apart. She got pregnant, and we decided to elope to Virginia Beach in April 1998. Why? This is a perplexing question. As it turns out, she *was* pregnant, but the baby was already dead. It would have been stillborn, and she knew this, but she refused to tell me until after the wedding. I found out by watching her voraciously consume alcohol on our wedding night. I learned the secret the next day. What was I supposed to do? A myriad of thoughts and possible actions ran through my head. She trapped me. To resume a previous analogy, she played me like an excellent fly-fisherman, until I was too tired to fight. Her presentation was flaw-less; she knew that I had morals and would never let a child come into the world without a solid foundation. Upon learning the truth, why did I stay with her? To this very day, I continue to wonder why.

It all had to do with the values that I possess and that I hoped that she had. When I said those marital vows, they meant some-thing to me. I could have, and—in retrospect—probably should have had the marriage annulled. The signs were there to see, but I had romantic blinders. We left Maine in her archaic Ford Escort, and we had a flat tire right after the George Washington Bridge in New York City—not a very pleasant location to stop, let alone be broken down. I went out to change the tire and discovered, to my amazement, that Lucinda didn't have a jack in her car. This should have been another sign from above for me to abandon this crazy notion of getting married. A Good Samaritan finally stopped to ask if we needed assistance, and he let me have his jack, and I changed the tire. At that time, I said to Lucinda, "Maybe we should turn around and go home."

She countered with, "It is us against the world." This appealed to my romantic notion of the American dream, and we decided to continue south toward Virginia Beach.

We arrived, acquired our marriage license, and got married. We only stayed in Virginia Beach for two days, and then decided to head back north to Maine. After getting married, I called my parents, and she called her parents to let them know. My parents never cared for Lucinda; they never trusted her. Her parents liked me because they knew her past, but they never had the courtesy to inform me about her history.

As it turns out, Lucinda was a convicted felon who spent time incarcerated. In fact, she was in jail when she was nine months preg-nant with Cassandra and would have given birth to her in jail if her parents didn't intervene to get her released. This was all news to me, which I didn't discover for five years. Her parents liked me because they thought I positively changed her toward the straight and narrow. Lucinda had an extensive criminal record in Alabama, New Jersey, and Maine that I never knew anything about. In brief, Lucinda was a convicted thief who stole money and merchandise—even from her parents. It seems to me that they should have let me know about her history. When I found out, I asked them why they didn't let me know, and their response was that she said that she had told me everything—lies! I didn't discover the truth until it was too late.

Upon returning to Maine, I went back to Madawaska to teach high school, and Lucinda returned to Lewiston and nursing. She had the stillborn baby removed and increased her visits to extreme northern Maine. I taught in a school that was located on the Canadian border. We often crossed the border into Edmonton, New Brunswick, to hang out. I would go skiing at Mt. Saint Anne and Lucinda would stay in the lounge. Before returning to Maine, we would stop at a bar and I was shocked to see some of my students there consuming adult beverages in various establishments. The drinking age was much more lenient in the Great White North.

I had a good job, and the pay was outstanding for two reasons. One, it was in northern Aroostook County, and they had to pay well to get people to go up there to teach. Two, Frazier Paper was located in town, so Madawaska had a large tax base, which helped fund local education. In terms of pay and security, it was a win-win situation, but I opted to leave Madawaska High School after one year.

Though I liked the location for its adjacency to the Allagash Wilderness Waterway, which had supreme fishing opportunities for brook trout and salmon, I chose to leave. I was no longer just thinking about myself. I was a married man. I resigned my position and moved back to my wife's area, Lewiston. We looked into buying a house, and my credit was outstanding. My wife's credit was less than stellar, which I wouldn't learn about for some years to come. We qualified for a mortgage for a manufactured home in Turner, Maine. The guy who owned the company owned the property on which the house was going to be placed, and he gave us a deal.

It was a picturesque location on a hill, with a breathtaking view of the adjacent mountains. I loved the view and the acre of land I got to play with. I planted grass and worked on clearing the stone wall in front of the property. The house was on a private road, with only three houses. We had to chip in with the other homeowners on the street to pay to have Valley View Road plowed during the winter months. This didn't cost too much, roughly seventy-five dollars each winter. It was new and exciting to live in a brand new house located on virgin soil. It felt like a key piece to my American Dream.

The house was a two-bedroom, one-bath Cape Cod style home with an unfinished upstairs. As the foundation was poured, we had to make a decision about how the house was going to be heated—oil-fired boiler with forced hot water heat, or a propane furnace. We mistakenly opted for the propane, because it was more economical, and we wouldn't lose any space in the basement or house to erect a chimney. This was a major mistake. Located on the side of a mountain, the house was pretty much always the victim of the prevailing wind. Manufactured homes aren't insulated all that well. Moreover, the people who erected it never installed an insulation barrier on the outside walls before installing the vinyl siding. Initially, the propane boiler *was* more economical, but the price of propane couldn't compete with oil. To keep the electric bill manageable, we opted for a gas dryer, which worked much better than the traditional dryer. I bought a generator and had it wired to the house in case we lost power, because we needed power to run the well and flush the toilet. All in all, we—or at least I—really liked the house.

I liked picking colors and painting the rooms in the house. We installed fancy railings to the unfinished upstairs, and I installed crown molding on all the ceilings. It was a bitch to do, but it looked really nice, which made me proud. As the house was growing and improving, so was our marriage. Soon after moving in, Lucinda became pregnant, and I was ecstatic. Things were really looking up. I was working for Proctor and Gamble and working seasonally at L.L. Bean. I applied for and accepted a teaching position at the local high school, Leavitt Area High School. I thoroughly enjoyed teaching world studies classes there, and I got along well with everyone who worked there—especially the principal, Nelson Beaudoin.

At this point in my life, I believed that I was living the American dream. I had a house, my 4x4 Toyota truck, my boat, a canoe, my fly rods, camping equipment, and a baby on the way. What else could I need?

I was really enjoying life—teaching school, accomplishing home improvements, and mowing the lawn. I bought a riding lawn mower, and like fishing, where my motto is that time on the water is time well-spent, I felt that time mowing the grass was time well-spent. Like most people, I think it is always better when it is bigger. That definitely applies to the lawn. I really liked making our lawn bigger and squaring off the land. It became a picturesque plot of land. Like my father, I really enjoyed spending time outside. I built an external stone fireplace to roast marshmallows and have campfires. With a baby on the way, I finished off the upstairs and created a huge bedroom with a walk-in closet for my stepdaughter. Lucinda's ex-husband, Arthur, never paid child support. Since I had a stable job, I paid for Cassandra's health insurance. In retrospect, I should have forced Lucinda to have her daughter covered by Arthur; moreover, he should have been required to pay child support. I was going through life with romantic blinders on.

Lucinda's pregnancy was fine. She worked up until a couple of months before giving birth to our son, who I named Camden James Richardson. I named him after a picturesque town in Maine. After Camden was born, I got him a basset hound, which I named Rockport. I couldn't wait to get home from work to be with Camden. I loved holding him, bathing him, changing his diapers, and playing with him. His first word was "DaDa!" This still makes me smile.

After giving birth, Lucinda did not return to Central Maine Medical Center. She got a part-time job working as a nurse in a nursing home. We agreed that we didn't want to have strangers raise our kids. In retrospect, this was much more important to me than her. As a teacher, I had summers off from teaching, and Lucinda would increase her work hours during this time. We began to socialize with our neighbors. Lucinda is much more social than me, and she and Cassandra were responsible for initially becoming friends with the Taylors, who are two of my best friends to this day. Cassandra made friends with Marissa Taylor, with whom she went to school in Turner. We met her parents, Aaron and Melody, through her, and we became friends with them. We had a lot in common with them. They had two children, too, and their children were from different relationships.

I made a trailer and put a hitch on my lawnmower. I would gather the family and put them in the trailer, and we would go visit the Taylors, who lived across Upper Street, which was the main street from which Valley View branched off. Aaron had a four-wheeler, and he got a trailer, and he would bring his family over to our house to visit us. We had a lot of fun together. Through them, we met their next-door neighbors the Lovejoys, and we too, became friends with them.

This wasn't good enough for Lucinda , because she wanted to be the alpha dog. She wanted to be in control of the neighborhood, and she played the neighbors against each other. I was just happy to have friends who lived nearby, so I could hang out with them and enjoy their company. Lucinda bought me a membership at the local golf club, Turner Highlands, and I played golf there. I had taken up golf when Lucinda and I got together because her father played golf at Fairlawn in Poland. I played with him a few times—not because I really enjoyed golf, but because it was the right thing to do. I wasn't very good at the links, but I was improving.

Lucinda didn't get me the membership because she wanted me to enjoy the sport; she wanted people to know that I was a member because it was a status symbol for her. She hoped to meet the affluent members of the community through me. I was not into that; once I discovered this, I didn't play too much golf. I did play a few times with my friends, and I did begin to like the game.

Lucinda became the cheerleading coach for her daughter at the local primary school. She became excessively proud and arrogant, and she would often flaunt to the community that she was an RN *and* the cheerleading coach. This wore thin on the Turner neighborhood.

Also, this was quite ironic, because she had lost her nursing license for lying on applications for nursing positions; she had never told her employers that she was a convicted felon and that her nursing license was on probation. Once this was discovered by the nursing home facility where she worked, Lucinda was fired. Again, this was news to me. She was fired from Central Maine Medical Center for the same reason. She got a job at an orthopedic facility as a secretary.

My mother worked as a unit clerk at Maine Medical Center, and she was told by a fellow worker that Lucinda had lost her nursing license. Mom informed me about this, but when I asked Lucinda about it, she lied, maintaining that she had her nursing license. Lucinda never told me the truth about why she lost her nursing license. She told me it was a paperwork error when she moved from Alabama to Maine, and that she would straighten it out. As a married man and a father of a newborn son, I believed my wife.

Teaching social studies classes at Leavitt Area High School was going well, and I had developed a reputation as a challenging and rewarding teacher. History classes were no longer frowned upon by the student body, but rather, they looked forward to them. This made me proud. I was also incredibly proud of my son. Camden and I did everything together. He was walking then, and I bought him a glove, and we played catch just about every day. He helped me do all my yard chores. We mowed the lawn together, and during the winter, Camden helped me clear the driveway. We built snow forts and had snowball fights. We were really bonding, and I thought that he would remember this for the rest of his life. I bought an old Two-up snowmobile, which Camden and I named Copper, after one of his favorite movies, "The Fox and the Hound." Camden loved to ride with me around our yard and neighborhood on Copper.

Lucinda allowed me to get the snowmobile because the Lovejoys had snowmobiles, and she wanted to get in better with them. The Taylors had a swimming pool, and we would often go over to their house on warm summer days and nights. I enjoyed spending time with both of my neighbors, but Lucinda would often badmouth the other neighbors when she was there. I discovered this one evening after snowmobiling with Mark and his wife. Lucinda and I were hanging out with the Lovejoys, and Lucinda was badmouthing the Taylors, and I would have none of it, so I made a scene and left. I went home, and Mark came over, and I told him in no uncertain terms that I vehemently disagreed with my wife and frowned on her behavior. Lucinda came home later, and we had a huge fight. I made it clear that I didn't want to see that kind of conduct again. I wanted Camden to accept all people as people, regardless of their backgrounds; kids get the majority of their personalities from their parents. This, however, didn't change her behavior, because later the Taylors had a yard sale, and Lucinda sold some things there that actually belonged to Mark's wife.

Was this foreshadowing? Camden was three years old, and the Taylors had a daughter, Sydney, who was four. They became friends. Camden was to start preschool soon, and I was excited.

I was beginning my third year teaching at Leavitt Area High School, and Lucinda and I were discussing whether or not to have another child. Lucinda argued that she didn't want to raise two only children. I maintained that we were raising two children, but there was huge age difference —nine years— between Camden and Cassandra. I agreed and prayed for another son; I had always wanted a brother, and I wanted one for Camden. Lucinda became pregnant, and once again, her pregnancy was uneventful. She gave birth to our second son in May 2001. Once again, I picked out the name: Bowdoin. Are you seeing a theme here? Yes, I love Maine. My sons are named Camden and Bowdoin. My cat's name is Rangeley, and my dog's name is Rockport. Why would I ever fathom leaving?

Florida

Lucinda had been talking to Melody who had decided to leave Maine and move to Florida where Aaron could get a better job and they could afford a much better house. This was a good time, economically, for real estate. Lucinda began casting her fly. It is truly ironic that she has never fly-fished, because she knows how to present the bug and make me rise to offer at her fly. Her artificial imitation was the concept of teaching high school in Florida. Lucinda convinced me that I could make much more money teaching in the Sunshine State. She argued that she could then be a stay-at-home mom. She played me well, because she knew that I was adamant that my kids not be raised by strangers. I forgot about her supposed nursing license. I swallowed the bait—hook, line, and sinker.

My respected principal at Leavitt left for Kennebunk High School, and he made it clear that he wanted me to join him there; we shared the same educational philosophy. I stayed at LAHS, and I let the school committee know that the teachers needed to be paid more. I got a stellar recommendation from Mr. Beaudoin, and I resigned my teaching position at Leavitt. We put our house on the market, and I prepared to leave for Florida. Our transportation situation complicated the potential move.

I had a 1994 Toyota truck, which I paid off early and loved. It was my second Toyota truck, and my first one had well over three hundred thousand miles on it when I traded it in for this one. Lucinda had her late eighties Ford Escort when we got married and moved into our house. The Escort was on its last leg, so we traded it in. Lucinda was pregnant with Camden at the time, and I continued to not use my brain. We bought a new Jeep Wrangler soft top, which was a nice vehicle but not all that practical for a growing family.

It was good in that it was an inline six cylinder four-wheel-drive vehicle. It was fun to drive in the summer, but it was rather cold in the winter. Lucinda initially liked the vehicle, and it was her idea to buy it, but she didn't like being cold driving it in the winter. We had two vehicles that weren't conducive to kids. After deciding again to have another child, we traded in our Jeep at the same dealership where we bought it and got a Nissan Quest minivan. After taking a huge financial loss, we now had a bona fide family vehicle.

After Lucinda gave birth to Bowdoin, she convinced me that my Toyota truck was not a practical automobile because it was not an extended cab, and it was impossible to fit two infant car seats in it. I traded it in to a used dealership for a 1993 Jeep Cherokee so I could bring the kids with me in my car. Was this an omen?

Melody and Aaron Taylor had already moved to Florida and were living in a place close to Tampa. I loaded up my Jeep with my clothes and teaching credentials and headed south. Meanwhile, Lucinda was researching houses and found a brand new Mercedes home online, which we would eventually buy. The only drawback was that it was located in Spring Hill, Florida. Upon arriving in the Sunshine State, I visited the Taylors, and they helped me find local schools where I could apply for jobs. They also helped me find a hotel and apartment complex where I could stay without signing a lease. It didn't take me very long to find a job; in fact, I accepted the first position for I which I interviewed. It was in a brand new high school located in Tampa. Its name was Freedom High School, and its mascot was the patriot, after the Super Bowl champions the New England Patriots, and in tribute to 9/11. My interview took place in a trailer, because the school wasn't finished yet. The principal and assistant principal were very impressed with me, and they offered me the job. My teaching certificate was transferrable to Florida, and they extended my expiration date for five years.

I informed Lucinda about the news, and our house in Maine had just sold, so she was getting ready to head south. Before departing Maine, Lucinda went crazy with the bills and charge cards, thinking that the companies would never find her or us. Entering into the marriage, my credit was top-notch. This was not the case for long. After getting married, I let Lucinda handle the bills because I was busy working, and when I wasn't working, I was engrossed in the lives of my sons—playing with them, bathing them, and feeding them. In short, being with them was paramount to me. Not keeping abreast of the bills proved to be a mammoth mistake, because Lucinda had a penchant for ignoring financial responsibilities.

Upon arriving in Florida, Lucinda stayed with me in the hotel, and the children stayed with the Taylors. It didn't take the builders long to finish our house, and we moved into it within a month. It was a large four-bedroom, two-bath house with a large living room, a dining room with a hardwood floor, wall-to-wall carpet, and walk-in closets. It also had a small, attached two-car garage. This was definitely an upgrade from our house in Maine. It sat on a little more than a quarter acre of land, which I mowed with a push lawnmower. Boy, I missed my riding lawn tractor. I did, however have a plethora of tools I brought down to Florida: power saws, drills, an air compressor, and hand tools—wrenches, sockets, and screwdrivers—all of which were important to me. I bought a workbench and ladders, which I strategically placed in the garage. Everything was neat and organized in my garage, but it proved difficult to park two vehicles in it, so I left my Jeep outside unless there was going to be violent weather—a hurricane. I really did like our Florida home. I liked the lanai, and the central air conditioning, which proved to be vital in Florida. The only terrible thing was my drive to Freedom.

Driving in Florida was much more hectic than driving in Maine. The traffic is outrageous, the road design complex, and Floridian drivers are less than courteous. I like to arrive to work incredible early. By contract, I was required to be at school twenty minutes before the first bell, which rang at 7:20 a. m. I usually arrived at Freedom between 5:30 and 6:00 a.m. for a multitude of reasons. The drive to New Tampa took between forty-five minutes to a little over an hour. I left early, so it was usually the former. I also liked to be at school early to prepare for the day's lessons and to finish any computer grading and administrative paperwork. It was common knowledge among my co-workers and students that I arrived to Freedom at an ungodly hour.

Students often took advantage of this and came to school early to receive extra help without their peers finding out. Freedom High School was like my alma mater, Yarmouth High School, in that it was an affluent, bourgeois, competitive community. Students wanted any academic assistance that they could get. I taught three advanced placement and three honors classes; these students were highly motivated. They brought in food and drinks, and we decided to start a breakfast club. We had a coffee maker and various breakfast foods. The most popular were Pop-Tarts. The club became incredibly popular, both from an academic and a social standpoint, and thus, I was proud of the breakfast club.

I always wore a shirt and a tie while I taught school, which I covered up with my sport jacket, which was a flannel shirt. This became famous at Freedom High School. It was odd to see anyone wear flannel in sunny, hot Tampa, but I wore a flannel shirt every day over my shirt and tie. Unlike schools in Maine, Freedom had a central air conditioning system, and I could control the temperature in my classroom; I kept it a comfortable sixty-eight degrees. Lo and behold—students began to wear flannel shirts in my classroom and around campus. This was unique in many ways. Since it was an affluent community, many students were dressed to the nines. This began to change when many students opted for flannel, because people couldn't tell how much money was in other people's wallets or purses by the clothes on their backs. This became the genesis for the flannel club, which I started with a couple of students.

We did fundraisers for those students who were less fortunate than their peers. Tampa had numerous high schools, and parents there could choose which school they wanted their kids to attend. Many students were then bused into New Tampa from less prosperous neighborhoods. Our flannel club assisted these students. After teaching an advanced placement world history class in my inaugural year, Freedom High School and I had developed quite a reputation—I had one of the highest pass rates in Hillsborough County.

There were more students in that one county then there were in the entire state of Maine. Once this news got out, many parents wanted their sons and daughters to come to Freedom. It was a win-win situation for me and for Freedom, because the next year, I got to teach more AP classes, which were incredibly challenging and rewarding.

Freedom was developing a reputation as a challenging and rewarding school, and more and more students were attempting to attend; therefore, the rise in student population caused a need for more teachers.

Teaching AP classes is a lot of work in terms of preparation. Numerous materials need to be collected and correlated, most notably original documents. They then have to be not only copied and dispersed, but an invigorating document-based question, or DBQ, must be designed. It was a ton of work, but I liked it. I attempted to finish as much of my paperwork at school so I wouldn't have to bring it home with me. Occasionally, this occurred, which pleased me because once I got home, I couldn't wait to be with my boys—to play games, read with them, bathe them, and feed them. It was so much fun. At night, I often watched movies with them, and once I put Bowdoin to bed in his crib, Camden and I would lie together in his bed and watch a movie until he fell asleep. This happened on a daily basis. Lucinda took advantage of this to have some time for herself, which I didn't mind; she was with the kids all day while I worked.

She often took the dog for a walk. At first, it was only for a half hour, but as time progressed, these walks became longer and longer. When I asked her about it, Lucinda would say that she had run into someone she knew. I didn't press her about this, but we really didn't know too many people who lived around us. In retrospect, I should have seen the writing on the wall.

Lucinda wasn't feeling well, and she went to the doctor. She had thyroid problems. She insisted that she had a lump on her thyroid and she needed some radiation therapy, which would make her "hot," so she couldn't be around the kids. Lucinda went through the procedure and had the lump removed. I was so thankful that she was okay. I saw her in the hospital, and she was fine and returned home in a couple of days. I didn't get a chance to discuss anything with the doctor. When I pushed Lucinda about this, she told me to be just grateful that everything turned out fine. Shortly thereafter, Lucinda said that she may have to go in to have further radiation treatments to ensure that the cancer hadn't returned. This was the first time that I heard the c-word, and I was petrified. A couple of months went by, and things returned to normal.

I came home from work one day in late August 2003, and Lucinda told me that she had just gone to the doctor and needed another high-intensity radiation treatment, so she couldn't be around Camden and Bowdoin for at least a week. I was a teacher, and I didn't have any vacation time or leave time to use, so I informed my parents in Maine. They offered to come down to Florida to be with my kids while I worked and Lucinda had her treatments. Once again, I resembled a fish that was expertly played by the fly-fisherman—in this case, fly-fisherwoman. Lucinda insisted that she would stay with Roxanne from the Catholic Church for a week while she was "hot." I bought the story—hook, line and sinker.

My parents arrived in late September to stay with us, and Lucinda left for her treatment. I was so proud to show my parents my house and all the work that I had done. They loved Camden's and Bowdoin's rooms, which I designed. Bowdoin's room had a fishing motif, even with a small fly-rod on the wall. Camden's room was blue with clouds painted on the walls. Both rooms looked very cool, and my parents were impressed with the house. They liked the large fence that I installed to enclose my backyard. It gave us privacy from our neighbors and a safe place for the kids to play.

Since it was Florida, and I am from Maine, I maintained that it never got cold in the Sunshine State. The boys and I would play outside on the Slip 'n Slide and in the kiddie pool. This pleased all of us, and I am proud that my parents got to see me play with my sons and that they could be with their grandchildren. This would all soon change.

Cancer Lie

Lucinda left to get her cancer treatments and to stay at the Catholic Church hospice facility … or so I thought. I went to work at Freedom High School, and my parents stayed with Camden and Bowdoin, who were then four and two, respectively. Work went well, and my parents took great care of my sons, who very much enjoyed being with their grandparents. When I got home from work on Monday or Tuesday, my mother had some interesting news to tell me.

She said that two men had called our house asking for Lucinda. Their names were Jason and Scott, and they both asked if Lucinda was there, and if she was married. I guess more than our dog's tail had been wagging during these long walks. It was a number of days before Lucinda called the house to talk with me, but she did call earlier in the day to speak with Cassandra.

I got in touch with the Catholic Church and spoke with Roxanne, who was flabbergasted by my questions and the corresponding news that I gave her. I asked her if I could speak with Lucinda, or at least have the telephone number of the hospice so I could communicate with my wife. Roxanne had no idea, no clue as to where my wife was. Moreover she didn't know anything about a cancer relapse. Why should she? It was all a fabrication, concocted by my deceptive wife.

Once I learned this, I again attempted to contact my wife by calling her cell phone. To no surprise, Lucinda refused to answer. I left a message telling her in no uncertain terms that the game was over, and that I knew the truth. Barely any time passed before Lucinda called me. I asked her where she was, and she responded, "At the Catholic facility." I told her that I had spoken in great length with Roxanne. Her tune began to change; she knew that she had been caught. I asked her where she really was, and she said a hotel. Lucinda continued to argue that she couldn't stay at the Catholic Church facility because she was too "hot" from the treatments. This time, the fish didn't jump, or even offer at the fly. I told her that her game was over, and that I expected her home soon.

A myriad of thoughts, emotions and questions were swarming around in my brain. My parents were obviously concerned for me and for their grandchildren. I wanted to learn many things. Clearly, I wanted to know what my wife was doing. The answers to those questions would have to wait. I also wanted to know why Lucinda had lost her nursing license, and I thought that was something my Mom could help answer. I convinced my parents to leave my house and to leave Florida — a titanic mistake. Lucinda arrived back home on a Wednesday, and to my mother's chagrin, my parents left the Sunshine State the following day. It had been quite a year for my parents. My Mom had decided to take my Dad back. She had decided that it wasn't her place to judge his actions. That would be forthcoming by a power greater than her. She actually adhered to her marriage vows, "for better or worse . . ."

Upon her arrival back to our Spring Hill abode, Lucinda and I exchanged unpleasantries, but she obstinately refused to answer my questions about where she had been, why she had been there, and whether or not she was alone. Initially, Lucinda attempted to stick with the recurring cancer argument, but her defense soon wavered. I made it crystal clear that I didn't appreciate being played for a fool. Moreover, I complained to her about how disrespectful she had been to me, to our children, and to my parents, who were in their late sixties and in no physical condition to be unnecessarily traipsing down to Florida under false pretenses.

My parents rushed back to Maine to research Lucinda's nursing license. Obviously, I didn't get too much sleep that night. I went to teach the next day. Upon my return home, the final nail had been driven in the coffin of our marriage.

The garage door wouldn't open, and the locks had been changed on my house. I pounded on the door, and finally, she let me in.

Lucinda announced to me that she had obtained a restraining order against me, and that I had to leave my home. What an absolute idiot I was. I once again swallowed the bait. I had done nothing wrong—nothing at all to warrant a restraining order. Also, it takes time and some evidence for any law enforcement agency to issue a restraining order. I just didn't think.

I gathered some clothes and left. Before I left, Lucinda poured salt in my wounds by admitting that she didn't have cancer, and that she was off with some guy—Lonnie—who she had met. Why couldn't she just have told me the truth? This question would continue to haunt me for the foreseeable future. It was a Thursday night, and I needed a place to stay. I found an affordable dump of a hotel to move into, located in a less than desirable part of town, but I had no options.

I immediately called in sick to Freedom High School for the next day. I basically spent the entire night on the phone. I called my parents, who were on their way back to Maine; I think I reached them in Virginia or in the Carolinas. My mother wanted to immediately return to Florida to assist me, but I told them to return to Maine. In retrospect, this was another immense mistake. If they had returned, they could have helped me acquire a lawyer, get my finances in order—cancel direct deposit of my paychecks and open up new bank accounts, and reenter my house to collect my personal possessions. As a history major and a history teacher, I know that "if" is the biggest word in history. Turning points, or lack thereof, revolve around that word.

I called Melody and Aaron Taylor and spoke with them about what was going on for hours. I also called my department head, Jill McEwen, to let her know that I wouldn't be at work tomorrow and to inform her about what was happening. She was resolute that I should stay with her and her husband. Jill was not just my department chair, but also a friend. I certainly needed a friend then. Jill, over the next week, would continue to insist that I stay with her.

The next day, I visited a lawyer—Thomas Einemann—and hired him to represent me. I called my parents to inform them of this, and they were literally just getting back to Maine. I gave them the lawyer's information and asked them to send a check to him so I could keep him on a retainer.

I went to the grocery store to get some food, and I basically just sat around in the hotel room and watched TV. As I said before, the hotel was located in a less than desirable neighborhood. A bunch of hoodlums were constantly milling around, yelling and swearing, and many were speaking a different language. This was petrifying for a sheltered country boy from Maine. I kept this to myself for a couple of days, because I didn't want them to worry more than they were already. Once I informed my parents about my situation, they agreed with Jill, and I told them and Jill that I would come live with her and her husband on Saturday, October 12 — if only I had. There's that word again … if . . .

The Accident

I called Lucinda to see if I could speak with my sons, and she let me. They said they wanted to see Daddy. I wanted to see them, too, so I asked them what they wanted to do, and Camden said, "Let's go to Chuck E. Cheese!" It was Sunday, October 12, 2003—the day that I was supposed to gather my things and go to live with Jill at her house in Valrico, Florida. Needless to say, I didn't, and this was a massive mistake as you will soon see. My kids have always come first, as I thought they should.

I had just been kicked out of my own house, the person I loved was in the midst of an affair, and I hadn't seen my kids in a week. Was I happy?

What makes me happy? By far, the most essential elements of happiness are my sons Camden and Bowdoin. I thoroughly enjoyed being with them and sharing life with them. I played with them and taught them things that they needed to know and things that were important to me, like fishing. Camden, Bowdoin, and I would often go fishing in the Spring Hill area, and we would all catch fish. To me, they were junk fish: crappies, bass, and sunfish—not the cold water species that I enjoyed landing, like salmon and brook trout. Those species, however, were nonexistent in Florida, for there was no cold water. At the time, it did not matter. All that was important was the smiles on my sons' faces when they got bites and landed their prizes. They both loved fishing with their Dad, and I was passing on something to them that was important to me, which is part of the American dream. This was being taken away from me.

I also enjoyed coaching my son's basketball and baseball teams. I coached Camden and Bowdoin in baseball and basketball through the local YMCA in Spring Hill, and I taught them how to swing golf clubs in our backyard and at the local driving range. We had tons of fun, but Lucinda also took this away from me. I arrived at my house in the early morning on October 12 to pick up my sons to take them to Chuck E. Cheese so I could spend time with them — so they could have some fun with their Dad. The establishment was over twenty miles away, and we ventured out. On the way there, Camden shocked the hell out of me by telling me that some guy was staying at our house. There was no one there when I picked up my kids, but once I learned this, I turned around and headed back home. I believe that I called Lucinda on my cell phone, and the rest I can't remember; I got in a substantial car accident, and I hit an eighteen-wheeler, flatbed truck.

To this day, I try to remember the catastrophe; I can't. All the information I have is from the accident reports, months after the event.

Bowdoin and I were airlifted to St. Joseph's Hospital in Tampa. Bowdoin had a broken leg. He was sitting in the back seat of the Jeep, behind me. Camden was fine physically; he had been in the passenger seat. I, on the other hand, was seriously injured, and the hospital personnel thought I was not going to make it. I suffered numerous injuries; I had brain swelling and was in a coma, and I had my left leg amputated above the knee almost immediately after arriving at St. Joseph's. I also suffered numerous internal injuries. No guy likes to talk about shrinkage, but in short — no pun intended — and my colon had to be shortened. For the next few months, I had a colostomy, on which I became fixated.

I woke from my coma, but the doctors reintroduced it because they were concerned about the brain swelling and brain shearing I was experiencing. I was in a coma for roughly six weeks. Upon becoming alert for basically the first time since becoming comatose, I saw a doctor at St. Joseph's Hospital on his knees, crossing himself and saying a prayer.

I learned later that Lucinda berated the doctor by saying, "Look what you have done to his sons." Basically, she was irate that the doctor removed my left leg — that he would let me live like that.

The doctor's response was, "At least now he will be part of their lives; now they will have a father." How little he knew about my wife.

While I was convalescing at St. Joseph's, my wife and kids were staying with Aaron and Melody Taylor—or at least that's what I was led to believe. It is true that my kids and dog were staying with the Taylors, but my wife was rarely there. Melody was nine months pregnant, and she didn't receive any assistance from Lucinda. This would have been understandable were Lucinda constantly by my bedside, but this was seldom the case. I learned about this through bank receipts for luxurious hotels, restaurants, clubs, and taverns that Lucinda frequented while I was battling for my life. Lucinda placed these expenses on our debit card; hence, I eventually discovered them.

I felt so bad for Melody and Aaron Taylor. The last month of Melody's pregnancy must have been cumbersome at best or hellacious at worst, taking care of my kids and dog, *and* her children, with no help from my supposedly grieving wife. I was in absolutely no condition to do anything.

In the middle of November 2003, after over twenty surgeries, St. Joseph's Hospital transferred me to Tampa General Hospital for in-house therapy. I hadn't been there long when the medical powers that be determined that I wasn't ready for or able to do the therapy. In December, I was placed in Heartland Nursing Home, located in Brooksville, Florida, which is contiguous to Spring Hill. Initially, I wasn't in very good condition. I had to wear a large, awkward neck brace all the time. If that weren't enough, I also had to wear a helmet 24/7. No wonder I didn't succeed in therapy at Tampa General!

I wasn't allowed to sleep in a bed; I had to sleep on a mattress on the floor. Initially, I longed for my catheter, but I got used to utilizing a urinal

My parents hadn't even been back in Maine for a month once they received news of my accident. They were at Lucinda's parents' home when her parents received a phone call from her, telling them the news. My parents were there trying to learn more information regarding the female dog.

My parents had contacted the state board of nursing about Lucinda losing her nursing license. She was placed on probation by the nursing board and only had to do a few things to maintain her nursing license, but Lucinda refused to follow protocol. The nursing board official, Myra A. Broadway, remembered Lucinda well and told my parents that she had never seen someone who was given so many chances to clear her name and retain her license. Ms. Broadway explained that Lucinda had numerous aliases and several Social Security numbers. The department of nursing had bent over backwards for my wife, but Lucinda refused to come clean with them, or, for the matter, with me.

While speaking with Lucinda's parents, the Holleys, my parents learned about Lucinda's criminal past—that she had stolen money and checks from her parents and from their neighbors, who later had her arrested. Lucinda was pregnant with Cassandra during one of her crime sprees, and she was caught and incarcerated for her thievery. In fact, she would have given birth in jail if her parents hadn't intervened and found some judicial sucker who agreed to release the female dog to her parents so she wouldn't have to give birth in prison.

Where was her husband, Arthur Philbrook? My parents learned that Lucinda had been married three times. That was news to me; I thought I was her second husband. Her first husband was a man named Puntolillo. She was arrested with him in New Jersey. Lucinda had criminal records in Maine and New Jersey, about which I knew nothing. Somebody should have told me. If not her, why didn't her parents have the decency to tell me about her? I don't know the answer to that question, so I can only speculate. They probably hoped that with my guidance, Lucinda had turned her life around. However, I wore blinders; I didn't know about her criminal past. *If* I had... there's that word again. If I had, I hope that I would have never married her.

If I had known, I would have definitely put a stop to some behavior of hers that I recently discovered during a joint shopping trip. On the bottom of the cart, under the basket, Lucinda had diapers, which she didn't place on the belt. At the car, I asked her about this, and she said she knew the diapers were there. She said that this was not the first time she had done this. I told her "never to do that crap with me again." If I had known about her criminal legacy, I would have been more forceful. I would have forced her to bring back the stolen property and tell the store that she discovered that the diapers were on the bottom of the cart, and that she hadn't paid for them. It was an honest mistake on my part, but I was unaware of her past. I didn't even learn about this until 2004; remember—it was December 2003, and I had just been placed in Heartland Nursing Home.

I don't remember too much from my early days in the nursing home, due to my colossal brain injury. I do recall one of my therapist's names there—Jennifer Cripe. She worked on my short-term memory. She made me remember my children's birthdays, which, at the time, I had difficulty remembering. Jennifer taught me to play memory games, which I mastered, and I taught her cribbage, which she believed to be a useful tool for my memory. We played cribbage on a daily basis.

I also called my wife daily to speak with her and my kids, but she often didn't answer the phone, so I left messages, which were never returned. I was not allowed to speak with my sons. This was a sign of things to come. It depressed me, so the nursing staff put me on an antidepressant drug, which I still take to this day. My wife rarely came to Heartland Nursing Home to visit me, and at first, my kids never came to visit me. Freedom High School raised exorbitant amounts of money—thousands of dollars—and gave it to Lucinda. What did she do with the money? This is a question that I still have; I have no clue what she did with that money or any of the other money that was coming.

She obviously wasn't paying any of the bills, and my house was threatened with foreclosure. I later learned that my friends from the park, Glenn Tulloch and Paul Hodgedon, sent her thousands of dollars upon learning about my tragic accident. I believe she used some of this money to temporarily save the house from foreclosure. Lucinda did not pay any of the bills that were in my name alone.

She never paid my cell phone bill or my automobile insurance bill. Ironically, I had written out a check for my insurance prior to my accident, but she refused to mail it. After my accident, she attempted to sue State Farm Insurance for not paying a settlement on my accident. I guess I was not the only one with memory problems, because she couldn't remember not sending in my insurance payment.

I was in so much pain—physical and psychological throbbing that would not end. In addition to my amputation, I had two steel rods inserted into my left forearm, and I had to wear a temporary brace. When not wearing the brace, I was supposed to use a high-tech, incredibly expensive device known as a bone stimulator, which was supposed to support bone growth around the inserted steel rods. I used the bone stimulator for a while, but the nursing home facility misplaced the device. They couldn't locate the stimulator, but one person who worked there thought that Lucinda may have taken it home with her from one of her rare visits. I didn't think too much about this at the time, but in retrospect, it does make perfect sense.

Lucinda never wanted me to get better, and with her medical connections, she could have easily unloaded the stimulator for a price. Lucinda worked for a doctor's office then, though she would soon be fired for illegally obtaining prescriptions. In addition to discomfort in my left arm, my right wrist throbbed constantly. I soon had an operation for that, and Dr. Hess basically said that I had suffered extensive damage to my wrist from the automobile accident, and I had to have it fused. I would never bend it again.

This ache was nothing compared to not being able to talk with and see my sons. I called my house one day, and someone answered the phone. It was a woman, but it wasn't my wife. This woman was babysitting my sons. Her name was Jasmine, and when I asked to speak with Camden and Bowdoin, she asked me who I was. I told her I was James Richardson, Camden and Bowdoin's dad. She said, "You're alive?"

I responded, "Yes, I am alive."

Jasmine continued, "I thought you were dead. Your boys were told by Lucinda that you were dead."

Again, I countered with, "I am very much alive, and I would like to talk with my sons." Jasmine saw the number of the Heartland Nursing Home on the caller ID, which corresponded to what I was telling her. After talking with her husband, Billy Fagen, they decided to bring my sons to see me at the nursing home.

I believe they initially did this without informing Lucinda. I was in my wheelchair in the lobby when they arrived, and I will never forget seeing my sons for the first time since my accident. I will never forget the first words I heard from them. They both yelled, "Daddy!" and Camden said, "I told you, Bowdoin, that Dad is not dead. He is alive."

I hugged them both and we talked for a little while. I was glad to see that they were both all right. Camden kept apologizing, "Sorry Dad...I am sorry."

I said, "Sorry for what?"

Camden said, "The accident."

I hugged him and gave him a kiss and told him, "No, no, no. You had nothing to do with the accident. I don't want to ever hear this again. That's why they are called accidents."

Once they left, I called Lucinda again, and she answered the phone. I decided to have a little fun, so I asked her where the kids were. She said that they were with her. I said, "Liar! They just left a dead man; even though I am dead, they looked great to me." She then hung up on me.

A couple hours later, she called me at the nursing home after learning the truth from the Fagens. I inquired about why Lucinda told my sons I was dead. Lucinda said, "They couldn't see you like that. It would be too traumatic."

I told her that was bull. They were so happy and relieved to see me. It was much more traumatic for them to be told that their father was dead. Now that I knew some of what was going on, Lucinda couldn't really sweep me into the dustbin of history, though she wanted to. I informed the nursing home nurses about what was happening, and they were supportive. All in all, it really sucked being in a nursing home.

I was in my late thirties, and I was by far the youngest patient at the nursing home. I had no one to hang out with or converse with who was from the same era. It was depressing. I had no leg, I was required to sleep on the floor, and I needed assistance getting from the floor to my wheelchair. Moreover, I needed assistance with daily living, which just about everyone takes for granted. I defecated into a colostomy bag that needed to be changed. The nursing staff refused to teach me how to change the bag, so I relied on them for this basic need. They also had to bathe me. They took me into a large shower in my wheelchair, hosed me down, allowed me to soap myself up where I could reach, and assisted me where I could not. Then, they would hose me down again to rinse me off. This weekly episode was completely humiliating.

I felt less than human. It was like I was prisoner of war. As a student of history, the only thing that came to mind to which I could relate the experience was the Holocaust. Like the Jews under Nazi hegemony, I too had no voice, no control, and no input about my daily life. All this had to change.

Lucinda purposely kept my parents in the dark. They had no idea where I was, and because of HIPAA laws, Lucinda had control of all the information about me. My parents' only information concerning me came from a less than reliable source. Lucinda told them that I was brain-dead, had to be fed, and that I could do nothing for myself. These were lies. She told her parents the same thing.

I had no contact with my parents. I would lie in bed and wonder where my parents were and why they had not contacted me. I had no idea that they were being fed false information. One December 18, after trying numerous times, I remembered my parents' phone number, and I had Teresa, a nurse at the facility, call them. They were so incredibly happy to hear my voice and to learn that I was not brain-dead. I told them where I was, and I gave them the number to Heartland Nursing Home. I informed the staff at the facility that my parents had my permission to be kept abreast of all information regarding me. I believe that I had to sign some form that spelled this out, because Lucinda would have never agreed to this.

She told my parents that I never asked for or talked about them. Once again—all lies. Despite all of this, things were beginning improve slightly at the nursing home. My mental state was getting better, and my short-term memory was getting better, and I was winning at the cribbage games.

I began to improve physically, too. Without a leg, I practiced "walking" around with a walker. It was more like hopping around, but at least it got me out of the wheelchair. Some of my colleagues at work came out to Brooksville to visit me. My department head, Jill, often came to see me, and occasionally she would bring fellow history teachers with her. It was nice to see my co-workers. This was the beginning of something miraculous.

Some of my students from Freedom High School ventured over forty miles from Tampa to visit me. They often brought gifts—cards, letters, and food. Their notes and words brought smiles to my face, and the food pleased my tummy—the food in the nursing home sucked. I had lost a lot of weight since the accident. At the time of the accident, I weighed 220 pounds, and in the nursing home, I was well under 140. I've seen pictures of myself during that time; I looked horrific. People said that I appeared withdrawn and looked like "all eyeballs."

One student in particular, Anjuli Lohn, came to visit me a few times. I called her Ms. Lohn; I called all of my students Mr. and Ms., followed by their last names. Since I started teaching, I did this for a plethora of reasons. Most notably, it gave all my students the respect that they deserved. As students, they had to call me Mr. Richardson, so I in turn gave them the same respect. Ms. Lohn would bring me Chicago-style hot dogs from her family's restaurant, Mel's Dogs. On one of her visits, she brought her father with her, and we talked about golfing. He said there was no reason why I couldn't play golf once I got an artificial leg. This gave me something to which I could look forward.

I repeatedly asked the staff at Heartland when I would getting a prosthesis. No answer. My health was basically okay, but I suffered from incurable heartburn. I took Prevacid, but it didn't seem to help. The indigestion got so bad that I vomited without mercy, so I was placed in Oak Hill Hospital, where they operated on me. They removed my gall bladder and reattached my colon. The doctors were skeptical about whether or not they would be able to do this, but they were successful on both fronts. I never thought that I would be so happy to defecate again. Nonetheless, I was happy to go to the bathroom like a normal person. Physically, things were definitely improving. Mentally, stuff with my wife and kids were basically the same. Occasionally, my wife visited me; a few times, she even brought Camden and Bowdoin to see me. This was extremely rare. Things would soon change.

My parents drove to Florida to see me in the nursing home, and my Aunt Joyce, Uncle Royce, Aunt Janice, and my cousin Jolene came as well. It was great to see my relatives. Once my relatives arrived, a strange thing occurred—my wife came to see me more often. Did she have a change of heart? No! Someone at the nursing home kept her informed about what was happening. One time, my parents came to visit, and they took me out to eat. When this happened, Lucinda came to the nursing home and rummaged through my belongings. Teresa caught her going through my personal belongings and told her that I wasn't there and asked her to leave. I am so glad she did, because my lawyer's papers were in a drawer right beside my bed—I was initializing divorce proceedings.

Lies
Discovered

Heartland Nursing Home was in the process of deciding whether or not to keep me as a patient. They held some hearings before my parents arrived in Florida, and my Aunt Joyce and Uncle Royce attended the meetings with me. My wife was a no-show. In brief, they said that Lucinda was attempting to gather funds so I could stay at the facility or obtain Social Security clearance, which would allow me to stay there. The nursing home said at that hearing that I would be allowed to stay. This was false.

I was also scheduled for my wrist fusion surgery. There was another meeting, and the nursing home said that after my surgery, I would need to find another place to stay. What had happened? I do not know; only conjecture, or educated conjecture, will have to do. I wanted to go home to my house in Spring Hill. I repeatedly asked my wife if I could come home. Her answer was an emphatic *no*. She said that she couldn't take care of me. With her background as an RN, this made no sense. I just didn't want to read the signs.

It was a good thing that my parents were there for me. Lucinda was with another guy; the guy she had been with, Lonny, had discovered that she was nothing but a liar. She told him that she needed money to fly to Maine and bury her mother, who had died. Lonny called my in-laws and discovered that they were fine—that no one had passed away. At least he found out the truth about her before it was too late for him. Lucinda was frequenting bars, and that's where she met Billy Fagen. Remember him? He, along with his wife Jasmine, was shocked to hear that I was alive when I called my house. They brought my kids to see me at the nursing home.

While out carousing and drinking, Lucinda met Billy Fagen and his business partner at Executive Curbing, Joe Kelley, with whom she hooked up.

Supposedly he didn't know that I was alive. Later, my father called Executive Curbing and spoke with Billy Fagen, who told him this. I tried to call my wife, but she wasn't home. She answered her cell phone and told me that she and the kids were at Disney World. What she failed to tell me was that Joe Kelley was with her. I later discovered this when I saw my bank statements, and there were numerous withdrawals from my debit account in the Orlando area. That's not all. Lucinda was later charged with grand theft in Orange County, Florida, for not paying her hotel bills. Lucinda was just adding to her criminal record in Florida.

Even this was just the beginning. While in the nursing home, I learned that Lucinda had purchased a new vehicle, a Land Rover. How could she afford a Land Rover? When I asked about this, she said that she got a great deal, and the sellers of the vehicle were aware of my situation. She said they felt badly, so she got a fantastic deal. I asked what was wrong with the Nissan Quest. Lucinda replied that it didn't run well and that it would take a lot of money to fix it. You guessed it again—nothing but a fabrication.

As it turns out, the minivan had been repossessed because Lucinda never paid the bill. Why should she have? It was in my name, so her credit wasn't affected at all. While in the nursing home, I received a large dismemberment insurance check from Standard Insurance. It was $17,000 check with my name—and only my name—on it. Lucinda forged my signature and deposited it into our joint account at Sun Coast Schools Federal Credit Union. She then purchased the Land Rover. Once I learned about this, I contacted Standard Insurance Company, and they told me it was part of my insurance policy as a teacher in Hillsborough County. The check was supposed to pay for a prosthetic leg.

The $17,000 easily covered the price of the used Land Rover. She spent the remaining $8,000 on herself. How, you ask? Lucinda spent the money for my prosthetic leg on her own body. She had her breasts augmented, but she was not done there. Lucinda had various scars removed and liposuction to remove fat. Evidently, this was much more important to her than obtaining an artificial leg for her amputated husband.

Before we moved to Florida, Lucinda convinced me to withdraw my money from the Maine State Retirement System so she could pay off her student loans. At the time, I didn't think to even question it. Upon coming back to Maine, I ran a credit check on her and discovered that she still had a hefty balance remaining on her student loans. She never used my retirement system money on her student loans. For what, then, did she use that money?

After copious amounts of research, I discovered that she had hired a lawyer to fight the loss of her nursing license. To make a long story short, this was a complete waste of my retirement account, because she lost her battle with the nursing board.

My parents arrived just in time to take me to my latest surgery, my twenty-third, if memory serves me right. This was my right wrist fusion surgery, which was performed by Dr. Hess. After the surgery, I wasn't allowed to go back to Heartland, so once I was released from the hospital, my parents took me to Aunt Joyce's residence in Winter Harbor, Florida. We stayed there a couple of days before heading north to Maine. While I was recovering from my wrist surgery, my parents and I went to the junkyard to see the Jeep's condition after the accident. Since I had no leg, and we were on irregular ground, it was impossible for me to go to my Jeep in my wheelchair. My parents went to the vehicle and took pictures of it; after seeing the film, I was amazed that I survived the accident. It is astonishing that Camden wasn't physically hurt at all and Bowdoin only suffered a broken leg.

I told my parents to get my fly rods, fishing equipment and golf clubs from my car. My possessions were not to be found. Obviously Lucinda had been there and took everything that she wanted from my car. The person at the junkyard told my parents that Lucinda had been there and taken everything that she wanted from my car, like the car seats. Afterward, we went to police station to ask some questions about my personal property, most notably my wallet. My father had asked Lucinda about my wallet, and she emphatically and repeatedly told him that she never got it.

My father spoke to the deputy in charge of my accident case. Dad asked him about my wallet. The deputy said he didn't have it—that he'd given it to. He told my father that he personally gave it to Lucinda, and that it had cash in it, over a thousand dollars that my parents had given me. Once again, Lucinda had lied.

My parents came to Heartland Nursing Home to take me to Dr. Hess for my wrist fusion surgery. I had the surgery, and we went to Aunt Joyce's house for a couple of days; then we drove to Maine. I was in a lot of pain from the surgery as we drove. I had a brace on my wrist, we arrived safe and sound back to my home state.

Return to Maine

I believe we arrived back in Maine in March or April 2004. I can't remember exactly, because of my brain injury, which even to this day impacts my memory retention capability. Let's recap a moment. I was back in Maine, living at my parents' home, without my left leg, without my sons, and without any source of income. In actuality, it was much more complex than that. My parents had to be terrified. They had to take care of an invalid. I was scared, too. How was I going to do what normal people take for granted? How was I going to be able to go to the bathroom on one leg? Take a shower? Get around the house? My Dad quickly worked on the house to make it handicap accessible.

He installed bars adjacent to the toilet and in the shower, which I could use to help with balance. I got around the house in my wheelchair, and I occasionally used my walker to hop around. My parents and I wished that the nursing home staff had taught me how to use crutches, but for some reason, they didn't. My father attempted to teach me how to use them. To a certain extent I can, but why bother when I have wheelchair? It is just much easier and safer to use the chair. I just wished that I was taught how to use crutches, because I have seen people get around well with one leg on crutches at Wal-Mart and other stores. Dad also had to install protective pieces of metal around all the door openings to protect the molding and paint from abuse from my wheelchair. I learned, after a while, how to navigate through the house without damaging it. Without my parents, I would have been a prisoner in that house. I couldn't leave the house or get into the house without assistance. I couldn't go up or down the stairs in my wheelchair. My father, who at the time was in his late sixties, had to basically take me in and out of the house in my wheelchair, which scared my mother and me to death.

I had to lean back in the wheelchair so my father could navigate the entry and the four steps leading up to it. I was terrified that I would fall backward into my father and hurt us both. I had to have trust, something that was sorely lacking in my life. This concept of lacking trust became a constant theme. Once I received an artificial leg, I had to trust it.

Occasionally, my parents liked to go out to eat, and they wanted me to go with them. Initially, I attempted to avoid these situations because I was self-conscious about my appearance. I am an amputee without an artificial leg, and I was embarrassed to be seen in public without my leg. I eventually gave in and went with them. Obviously, I needed help getting in and out of the vehicle; specifically, I needed assistance getting from my wheelchair to the car seat and vice versa. While I was in Florida at the nursing home, I only went out in public twice. The first time was when Jill came to visit me. She took me out to get away from the nursing home. The second time was when my parents came down to see me. In brief, I didn't like people seeing my stump. I was embarrassed. I had to change my outlook, but that was easier said than done. In the back of my mind, I thought it would be much better if I had an artificial leg. My brother-in-law Michael Loconte researched prostheses, and through him, I got in contact with John Paul Donovan of Atlantic ProCare.

To this day, I have my brother-in-law to thank for John Paul Donovan, or J.P. When I first met J.P., he examined my stump and didn't like the size of it. For a few weeks in May 2004, I had to wear a shrinker to minimize the size of my stump. In June, J.P. cast me for my first socket, which is the thing that connects my stump to my artificial leg. J.P. got me a state of the art prosthesis known as a C-Leg. I believe the C stands for computer. Believe it or not, there is a small computer in the knee of this artificial leg.

Through this process, I learned some new terminology. I was an AK—above knee—amputee, but I wished that I was a BK (below knee) amputee. It would have been much easier to learn how to use the artificial limb if I still had my knee.

No one who works with amputees uses the word stump. They call what's left of my leg a "residual limb," not a stump. It took me a while to use this term, but to be politically correct, I now use the term residual limb rather than stump. J.P. said that I have a short residual limb and that it would be much easier, from his perspective, to fit me for my prosthesis if my residual limb were longer.

I figured I would just strap on the device and start walking. How incredibly wrong I was. I had to put a special liner over my residual limb that had long type pin that resembled a screw. I had to learn how to put this liner on first. It is made of a pliable rubber, and you just don't pull it on; in fact it can't be pulled on. It has to be rolled on. I quickly learned how to do this, and then I had to learn how to get into the socket. I had to line up the liner so that the pin would be able to hit a hole. This was also much easier said than done. J.P. drilled a large hole on the outside of my socket so my father and I could see into the socket to see if the pin was lining up to the hole. Once it was lined up, I would then press down and get clicks from the screw like pin thing. Once I heard a few clicks, my leg was safely attached. At times, I had to stick a screwdriver into the hole to pull the pin toward the hole. J.P. was vehemently against this technique, but you have to do what you have to do to be able to walk. I was sick and tired of being stuck in a wheelchair.

I assumed that once I strapped the leg, on I would just start walking, but because of the harrowing nature of the accident and the ensuing traumatic brain injury, I had to learn how to walk again. In this sense, I was similar to an infant learning how to walk for the first time. Initially, I used a walker to help me stand up and get around. John Paul set me up with therapy at Saco Bay Physical Therapy, and with their help, I learned how to walk again. I learned how to walk inside parallel bars and behind a walker.

J.P. consistently told me that I had to trust the leg. In layman's terms, when I walked, I had to place all my weight on my artificial left leg when I took a step with my real leg. Initially, I would step quickly and hike my left hip; I did not spend enough time on my left leg. I practiced a lot at therapy, and Dad had our friend Paul Mac-

Donald, who is a welder, build us our own parallel bars. Dad placed them in our garage so I could practice at home. A couple of months went by, and I my walking got better and better.

I graduated from a walker to a cane, and I spent enough time on my prosthetic side to make my prosthetic knee bend. I wanted to thank J.P. and Atlantic ProCare for everything that they had done for me, and I made this clear to J.P. Together, we contacted WCSH, local channel six, and they decided to do a news story on me. Vivian Leigh, a reporter, came to Atlantic ProCare to interview me. A camera man filmed me walking on a treadmill and going up and down stairs. This appeared on the local news, and I received a copy of the story. I also taped the news that night. I sent a copy of my story to my sons so they could see their Dad walking.

I hadn't spoken with my boys since leaving Florida and returning to Maine. I had filed for divorce from the female dog, and once this occurred—lo and behold—Lucinda called me. I asked to speak with Camden and Bowdoin, and she let me. She said that she was now working, and the kids were in preschool, but she refused to tell me which school. After much research, I discovered that they went to Scribbles. I called Scribbles, and they were shocked to hear from me, because Lucinda had told them I was dead. Once I proved to them that I was indeed the boys' father, I was put on my sons' records as an emergency contact person. While in Maine, I kept in contact with Jill McEwen about my progress. Jill told me that my job at Freedom High School was still mine—that the principal, Richard Bartels, was holding the job for me. They had given me an extended leave of absence. It was now August 2004, and the school wanted to know if or when I would be coming back to work. As you can see, I had a lot to digest.

J.P. and my therapists at Saco Bay didn't want me to go anywhere until I learned how to use the leg. I still really couldn't walk that well without the use of my cane. In retrospect, I should have listened to J.P., but I didn't. With the proceeds from the "Race for Richardson," which was a race held on my behalf before I left Florida, I bought a 1995 Chrysler LeBaron convertible and got MapQuest directions to Florida. I was finally going to live with Jill and her husband. The school year had already started in Florida; then, they started much earlier than Maine.

Before departing Maine in September, I contacted my lawyer, Mr. Einemann, and my sons. I informed Mr. Einemann about the money Lucinda had received from Freedom High School and the signature forgery on my dismemberment check, and I sent all the corresponding paperwork that proved the amounts of money Lucinda received. I called my sons to see if they had received the tape of me walking on the news. The female dog told me that her parents saw me on the news, taped it, and sent it to her. I have no idea about whether or not the in-laws sent anything, but I know that I did. I spoke with Camden and Bowdoin, and they were happy to talk to me and to see me on TV. I missed them so much.

My Children

I had lost so much time with my sons. At the time of the accident, they were only four and two. To this day, I can still see them coming into the nursing home to see me in my wheelchair. I can still hear Camden saying, "I told you, Bowdoin, that Daddy is not dead." I wanted them to see their Dad out of a wheelchair. My accident impacted everyone in the Richardson household. Because of Lucinda, my parents have no relationship with my sons. I can't believe a human being could be so mean.

In December 2004, my parents and my sister sent presents to Camden and Bowdoin. They were opened, then rewrapped, and sent back with the following message: "Refused to accept." They were all opened so the female dog could look for money. There was no money—just gifts, notes, and messages for my sons. This hurt my sister and continues to hurt my parents and me. How could Lucinda be so callous? My parents also sent gifts from me from Maine; they were also returned. That I could no longer send gifts to my kids hurt me so much.

I wanted to give them something. I *had* to give them something. I wanted them to know that their Dad hadn't forgotten them—that their Dad would never forget them. I decided to get them savings bonds in their names and mine so she couldn't cash them in and spend the money on herself, which I know is exactly what she would have done if given the opportunity. I refused to give her that opportunity.

I miss them both so much. It hurts! Basically, all I have are my memories of them. I remember more about Camden than Bowdoin because I had more time with Camden. I remember our house in Maine, where Camden would help me work around the yard. We would mow the lawn together, and he would help me rake the yard and work in our garden. We would ride our snowmobile, Copper, around, and we would go and visit the neighbors together. I coached Camden in baseball and basketball in Florida, and I played basketball and baseball with both of them in our yard. We all hit baseballs off of a tee, and Camden and I often played catch. I loved being with my kids and playing with them. My sons were more than an integral part of the American dream; they *became* the dream for me.

Camden and I also liked to throw the football around, and we—being guys—roughhoused around by playing tackle, which Camden loved to do. Bowdoin was too young to tackle, but around the time of the accident, we had started to play that way, too. This is so sad; I doubt that Bowdoin can remember this or anything about his Dad. I am a grown man, and I am not afraid to admit that I often cry when I think about this. It makes me so sad, and I have a feeling of helplessness that I can't overcome. Is there any wonder the doctor prescribed a "happy pill" for me?

I would do everything with them. I, not Lucinda, bathed them. I took the blades out of razors, and we lathered ourselves up and shaved together. They loved doing this. We watched TV and movies together; we especially enjoyed *Scooby Doo*. I also read to them on a daily basis. Camden and I often fell asleep together. In short, they thoroughly enjoyed spending time with their Dad, and they couldn't wait for me to get home from teaching school. This was true for me, too.

Like any father, I introduced them to things that were important to me. I taught them how to fish. I bought them both fishing poles and took them fishing, and it pleased me to no end that they both loved it. They always asked, "When are we going fishing?" When we lived in Maine, I took Camden out on my boat, and we went fishing together. I had to sell it when we moved to Florida, and my wife said at the time that we'd get another boat first thing when we got settled in Florida. Did we get another boat? I think that you know the answer to that question by now. Before leaving for Florida, Lucinda made me sell all of my Maine gear, camping equipment, my tent, my sleeping bags, stove, lanterns, and some fishing paraphernalia. What was happening to my American dream?

They had fun, and I had fun doing things with my sons that we all enjoyed. Once Camden and I found a place to fish, we checked it out to determine if it was a good, safe location to bring Bowdoin. Remember that Bowdoin was only two years old. I didn't want to fish in a location that was potentially hazardous to the health or safety of my kids. I had to ensure that the spot wasn't conducive to the prospect of falling in the water. Unlike Maine, the water in Florida was potentially dangerous due to some of the critters that lived there, like alligators. Kids are fascinated by gators, which are quite numerous in Florida, as it is a state basically built on a swamp. Since the University of Florida mascot is the gator, the creatures are incredibly popular with children. While fishing, we occasionally saw alligators, and I had to restrain Camden and Bowdoin, who wanted to get too close to them for my liking.

Before losing my leg, I went fly-fishing once in a stream for junk fish. I was wearing waders and casting and catching bass when something out of the corner of my eye caught my attention. You guessed it—a gator was floating around upstream toward the other side of the river. I was fishing popper flies, and the prudent move would have been to exit the water immediately. Did I? No. I am a decent fly caster, and I liked the challenge of man versus beast. I casted a popper fly toward the alligator, who submerged himself and came over to the fly to check it out. He nudged it, and as I stripped the fly line in, he started to follow it. I quickened my retrieval pace and brought my fly in. At this point, I realized that I was not the sharpest tack in the box. The gator was within twenty-five feet of me. I got the hell out of the water quickly. I never brought my sons river or stream fishing. When I took Camden and Bowdoin fishing, we would pond fish, and I always scouted out potential fishing spots to ensure that they were safe for my sons.

Once I finally received an artificial leg and returned to Florida, I took my sons fishing once around Freedom High School. Bowdoin caught a big largemouth bass, and he was tickled to death. I have missed so much time with my sons. I missed their first days of school, their extracurricular activities—Bowdoin's karate and Camden's football and baseball games—and this hurts me so much. Not day goes by that I don't think of my sons. I wonder if they are okay, if they are thinking of me, and what they are doing. Lucinda refuses to keep me informed about the lives of my sons. She never sends me pictures of my sons, let alone pictures of Camden and Bowdoin in their team uniforms, or even their school pictures. She refuses to follow the divorce decree.

Back to Freedom

I left Maine in late September 2004 to return to teaching high school social studies classes in Tampa. I followed my Map-Quest directions and drove my old LeBaron straight through to Florida. The tricky parts of the journey were New York around the George Washington Bridge and around Washington, DC. It was much more difficult for me to travel this time, with an artificial limb. I brought teaching clothes — dress shirts, pants, and ties. I also had regular clothes for Floridian weather, which included shorts, T-shirts, and swim trunks. I had some teaching materials — grade books, plan books, and whatnot. I included my wheelchair, cane, and a TracPhone for my travels.

I drove to Florida almost nonstop — only stopping for gas and bathroom breaks that I couldn't take in my car. I made the journey in a little less than twenty-four hours. Needless to say, I made out-standing time; that pace was ridiculous for someone in my condi-tion, but I wouldn't learn from that experience.

Before departing the great state of Maine, I was in continuous contact with Jill. I sent her daily lesson plans for my AP world his-tory, honors world history, and honors philosophy classes. I did this with the hope that I could hit the ground running once I returned to teaching at Freedom High School. At times, I had to remember that I was an amputee, and it was difficult — if not impossible — for me to run. Since I didn't know exactly where Jill lived, I drove to Freedom High School and called to tell her I had arrived in the Sunshine State. She drove to meet me, and I followed her back to her house in Brandon.

I met her husband, Louis Sicona, and his brother or half-brother, Kenny, who was living there. I didn't know that Kenny lived there. Jill, being foolish, was under the erroneous assumption that

I wouldn't stay there if the house was crowded. Jill knew me well and was aware that I had antisocial tendencies, for at work I rarely socialized with fellow faculty/department members but rather spent all my time with students, but she was wrong on a few fronts. First, her house was huge. Second, I really took a liking to Kenny, and we became friends. Finally, I had no other options but to live with Jill, and I think somehow she may have forgotten that. I am so thankful to this very day to Jill and Louis for everything they have done for me. They are and will be forever in my prayers.

I started back to work the following Monday at Freedom High School. For the first couple of weeks, I left my car at Jill's and rode to work with her. I received an elevator key because my classroom was on the second floor. I brought my cane, on which I relied heavily to get around. The students were amazed and glad to see me back, doing what I loved. Two students in particular were so happy to have me back — Claire Forbes and Stacy Hall. They had made me a plaid quilt that I still use to this day as my blanket. Many of the students once again began wearing flannel shirts and flannel swatches, which had been sold as part of a fundraiser for me. The breakfast club started back up again, and students arrived to Freedom very early to have coffee and breakfast with me. Once the breakfast club started again, I drove my own vehicle to Freedom; these students and I arrived to school much earlier than Jill. They came to school to receive extra guidance and help on their AP and honors assignments, and to hang out with me, so I had to be there early. Besides, I enjoyed getting to work early. I often arrived at Freedom High School at 6:00 a.m. or even earlier. Students began arriving a little after six.

Jill was incredibly supportive of my work endeavors. Often, I left her abode before she had even gotten up. She helped me whenever I needed it at work by bringing me my school mail so I wouldn't have to struggle to the office to get my own. She assisted me in setting up the school's grading system, Grade Quick. Often, students would also help by taking my correspondence to the proper destinations so I wouldn't have to traipse across campus.

Because of my physical limitations and my brain injury, I was nervous about teaching again. Before the accident I was always prepared for the daily lessons, but now I was initially quite anal about being prepared for the daily activities. I wrote everything down in notebooks for each class, which I never did before the accident. This was now part of my daily routine. I just didn't want to forget anything. I still suffered from short-term memory problems, and this alleviated those problems. I quickly recaptured some of my old glory, and the job became easier and easier. In terms of administrative stuff, Jill reminded me of upcoming deadlines so I could meet them. The first couple of weeks were a transition period for everyone.

My fellow teachers, except Jill, were skeptical about whether or not I could perform at the high level I had before the accident. For them, I was kind of an anomaly. I had extremely high standards and worked my students beyond comparison, yet I was incredibly well-liked and popular among them. This perplexed and confused many of my colleagues. Except for philosophy class, in which I had many students that I had known before my accident, the transition was arduous. Those students had adjusted to the expectations and standards of the person who had replaced me.

Even though the first quarter was almost half over upon my return to Freedom in late September 2004, I started as though it were day one of the year, with meet and greet activities, so students could get to know me and I could get to know them. I went over all my expectations for them and the various ways for them to meet those expectations. Since I rely heavily on writing in all of my classes—I am convinced that every class is an English class—I began by teaching students the six-paragraph essay. I taught them how to write an engaging introduction and three body paragraphs that defend the thesis, which is the integral component of the introduction. In brief, I taught my students that writing a historical essay is similar to a lawyer arguing a case. Lawyers' opening statements are similar to the introduction; the case itself is congruous to the body paragraphs. We are now up through four paragraphs and here is where I differed from the English department which favors the five paragraph essay.

Paragraph number five, for the English department, is the conclusion. I vehemently disagree, and this is something completely new for the vast majority of my students. I taught my students to write a concession paragraph for their fifth paragraph. In this paragraph, students mention the opposing point of view, which proves to the audience that they know more than their own perspectives. If they do it well, then they will attack the opposing standpoint, which in turn validates their theses. Paragraph six is the conclusion, and I told my students that it is similar to a lawyer's closing arguments. I believe that this is the most vital part of the essay—their last chance to verify their theses. Unlike lawyers, I encouraged them to save their most prominent evidence for their closing argument. The AP graders seemed to like this approach; my students scored well on their exams. In fact, I had one of the highest pass rates on the AP exam in Hillsborough County.

I got along quite well with Jill and her husband, and Kenny became a close friend of mine. He helped me get a real cell phone to replace my TracPhone. Due to my marriage and my wife's refusal to pay any bills when I was in the nursing home, my credit was in shambles. I had to get a lawyer and declare bankruptcy. I also had to go to Hernando County for my divorce proceeding in November 2004. My lawyer, Thomas Einemann, did a horrific job representing me. I had been in constant contact with him while I was in Maine, and again when I returned to Florida. The mortgage company had begun foreclosure proceedings on my Spring Hill home. I went to court twice in an attempt to force Lucinda to sell my house so I wouldn't lose all the equity. At first, the judge refused to make her put the house up for sale. The second time I went to court, the judge finally realized that Lucinda wasn't going to make any mortgage payments, even though he issued court orders telling her to do so. A "For Sale" sign was placed on my house, and Lucinda allowed me to pick up some of my belongings, which didn't amount to much more than spit in a bucket. I went there with Jill and Kenny; we took two vehicles, but all I got easily fit into one car.

I took two saws and some hand tools that were mine, but I didn't get my workbench, air compressor, ladders, or ramps. I didn't even get all my fishing equipment—most notably my fly rods, spinning rods, or my saltwater equipment. She even kept the majority of my flannel shirts. Anything that meant something to me, she kept. Lucinda didn't even give me any baby pictures of my sons. How could anyone be so hurtful? I never did anything to harm her.

Lucinda wasn't at the house when we went, but it was locked so I couldn't go in to look around. I am sure she sold everything that I wanted in garage sales. I told her what I wanted before driving over to gather my things, but none of the things that I mentioned to her on the phone were on the front lawn when I got there. Basically, in seven years of marriage, I couldn't even fill a small duffel bag with the remnants. I made this point abundantly clear to Mr. Einemann, but he did nothing in the divorce proceedings to attempt to rectify this situation.

In November, I took a day off so I could get divorced. I wanted a divorce trial so I could fight for everything that was stolen from me. Mr. Einemann argued against this. I wanted all the money Linda had stolen—all the money raised by Freedom High School and the $17,000 dismemberment check Linda had cashed. My lawyer argued that this money would count against unpaid child support, which hadn't been paid since my injury and for future child support over the next two years. He argued that things might be worse for me if I had a jury trial. By my calculations, the money in question was more than $35,000. In retrospect, I should have opted for the jury trial, but I listened to my lawyer's counsel.

I went to trial, and Judge Curtis Neal granted my divorce with the following stipulations, which weren't worth the paper on which they were written on: I was to have my sons every other weekend and every other holiday on a rotating schedule. I was also to have my sons for six weeks during their summer recess from school, and during their school vacations. This all amounted to a bucket of spit, because Lucinda never followed the divorce decree. When I informed Mr. Einemann about this, he said that I could spend thousands of dollars to take her back to court, where the judge would slap her on the wrist, but she would probably only temporarily adhere to the divorce decree. Nothing would be in put in place to force her to follow it. My only option was to fight for full custody of my sons. At the time, this wasn't an option for me. I was just learning how to get around on my artificial leg, and I had just declared bankruptcy by no fault of my own.

Lucinda and I were divorced in November 2004. The first holiday, Thanksgiving, was fast approaching. Lucinda didn't put up much of an argument when I asked to have Camden and Bowdoin for Thanksgiving that year. Jill and Louis put out a nice spread, and my sons had fun with their Dad. We played together outside, and for the most part, I got around quite well on my leg; I only fell once. I fell while holding Camden up outside so he could look over the fence. I will never forget what happened. Camden wasn't hurt at all, and he was so concerned about hurting me. He helped me get up and apologized for making me fall. He didn't make me fall! I told him that it wasn't his fault. After playing outside, we watched TV together and had a great weekend. In the back of my mind, I wondered why Lucinda hadn't put up much of a fight about me having the boys over the Thanksgiving holiday.

As it turned out, Lucinda really didn't have much of a choice. She had to be in court in Orange County to face grand theft charges. I didn't know about this at the time; I found out via Internet. She wasn't being nice to me by letting me be with my sons; she had no choice. This was just the beginning of several legal troubles.

What happened to that American dream? I was no longer in love or married—thank God—but I was also not the integral component of my sons' lives, which I wanted to be. As a father and a believer in the American dream, I desired to give my sons an environment and tools that would enable them to avoid the mistakes life would throw at them, or at least the mistakes I made. Lucinda refused to let me be part of their lives. See appendix A.

I was teaching high school students, being a positive influence in their lives. They, in turn, were an encouraging power in my life. The teaching dress code was a bit more lax in Tampa than it had been in Maine. I almost always wore a dress shirt and tie, covered by my flannel sport jacket, and I was dressed much more professionally than the majority of my co-workers. Instead of dress pants, however, I opted to wear shorts, which revealed my artificial limb. When the administration asked me about this, I told them that it was easier for me to get around with shorts on, because I could monitor whether or not the artificial knee was behaving correctly. At best, this was a half-truth. It was, and is to this day, psychologically easier to move around with shorts on. It is much easier to get dressed in the morning with shorts rather than pants; pants are more difficult to get on over my prosthetic limb and more time-consuming. I am not bashful or ashamed of my artificial leg, and I wanted my students to know and understand that. Why attempt to hide it?

Besides the breakfast club, many students chose to bring their lunches to my classroom and eat with me rather than in the cafeteria. I had always chosen to eat lunch in my classroom rather than in the teachers' lounge, even before becoming an amputee. Students did this for a number of reasons—to receive extra guidance on assignments, or to just shoot the bull. It gave the students an adult presence that many lacked at home. We all benefitted from this in many ways. Once we finished our lunches, if I didn't have any last minute paperwork to complete, some students would take me outside of the classroom to practice walking without the cane.

They monitored my leg to ensure that I was bending the knee properly. Instead of using the elevator, they suggested that I try the stairs. As I challenged them, they challenged me, and I wanted to be a good example for them. Besides, I wouldn't let them duck my challenges in the classroom, so how could I avoid theirs? I walked down numerous flights of stairs without my cane, and I have them to thank for teaching me and believing in me. It was easier to walk in Florida than it is in Maine. It was somewhat easier to walk on the flat cement walkways around campus, so the students put me on the grass and made me walk on irregular ground, which both scared and challenged me. Sure—I fell a couple of times, but they were there to help me get up. All in all, my mobility improved drastically. Things were looking up.

Then, one day, as I was walking down Jill's driveway, my knee gave out. I fell hard and broke my collarbone. This had significant ramifications for me. I couldn't wear my leg; it didn't work. The knee wouldn't support me or bend when it was supposed to. I contacted John Paul Donovan, and he used his connections to find someone I could see in Florida to work on my prosthetic limb. They sent my C-Leg away to be fixed and gave me a loaner leg to use until mine was repaired. This all took over a week to accomplish, so I was stuck in wheelchair for a week. Jill had to take me to work in her car and help me get into the wheelchair from the car and vice versa. It was incredibly scary to teach and maneuver around a high school campus in a wheelchair. The hardest thing to do was to go to the bathroom. After doing this for over a week, I had a much more profound respect for disabled students.

Once I got my leg back from being repaired, I developed a lot of bad habits because I had lost faith in my leg. Before the accident, I had been told from day one that I had to trust my leg, which meant that I had to put all my weight on it when I took a step with my right leg. I did this before falling in Jill's driveway, but after my artificial knee gave out and I broke my collarbone, I suffered psychological as well as physical damage. In terms of walking, the psychological impact from the fall was much more severe. I really had a hard time trusting the leg. Instead of spending enough time on the artificial side so I could swing my right leg through, I stayed on my left side just long enough to step with my right foot. I didn't even realize that I was doing it. I guess there is a huge difference between stepping and walking; I was no longer walking, just stepping. In doing so, I hiked my left hip so I wouldn't have any flow. My gait suffered tremendously. I got into some physical therapy in Florida, and they attempted to work on that, but I didn't improve my gait until I got back to Maine, which didn't happen until the summer of 2006.

During the fall, I also landed on my right, fused wrist, which caused significant damage. I had to have that wrist re-fused by the same doctor that originally operated on it in January 2005. I had been talking to Jill about moving out of her house and finding a place to live on my own so I could spend more time with my sons. It wasn't easy for me to find a place to live—remember, my credit was in shambles due to my ex-wife. Jill found me place to live near her in a neighborhood called Bloomingdale Woods.

It was a small, one-bedroom apartment with a tiny kitchen. Jill and Louis gave me a bed and some dressers, and a fellow social studies teacher, Tiffany Ewell, gave me a couch and chair. Jill also gave me a microwave from school and an old coffeemaker from Freedom, which, ironically, I originally donated to the history department.

In brief, I had the essentials to start out on my own. My parents drove to Florida to help me move into the new apartment, and while they were there, they helped me buy a new car. The old LeBaron was on its last legs. The power windows wouldn't even work. My father had to cosign because my credit prohibited me from obtaining a loan on my own. I bought a brand new 2005 Hyundai Elantra in January 2005. Thanks, Mom and Dad. Teaching went well that year, and once again, my students performed majestically on the AP world history exam. At the end of the academic year, I returned home to Maine.

My sons were in Maine, because my former in-laws had taken them when Lucinda was arrested again—for numerous reasons. She was arrested at Scribbles Daycare for not having the right license plates on her car. She failed to register her new Land Rover. Instead of registering it, Lucinda used the license plates from the minivan, which had been repossessed. She was also arrested for theft charges.

Lucinda has never had a problem writing checks, but she has a long history of having a problem backing those checks up with cash in the bank. Lucinda biggest crime was grand larceny in Orange

County, and then failure to appear in court in Hernando County. She was incarcerated for these crimes, and my in-laws sent money to Florida to fly my sons to Maine while she was imprisoned. Camden and Bowdoin had been in Maine for a month.

I learned all about this from Vanessa Farnworth, who picked up my sons at Scribbles Daycare. I also learned from her that Lucinda had been working at Miss Kitty's, an establishment where she wore low cut shirts—or no shirt—to show off her augmented breasts. Vanessa told me that Lucinda was fired by Dr. Schwayb Oak Hill Hospital for stealing and altering prescriptions. I also learned from Deputy Ross at the Hernando County Sheriff's Office that Lucinda was evicted from her Wiltshire Avenue apartment and had to go to court because the landlord wanted the rent that Lucinda never paid.

I got to Maine at the end of May 2005, in time for Bowdoin's fourth birthday. My parents and I went to the Holley's house to celebrate Bowdoin's birthday. Camden and Bowdoin were so happy to see me, and I was pleased to see my sons. The Holleys brought Camden and Bowdoin to my parents' house on June 1, 2005, and they stayed there with me. We had so much fun together, riding four-wheelers, fishing in the Royal River and seeing all the wildlife. Bowdoin loved seeing the deer come to my parents' house to be fed. They were so tame, and both boys, especially Bowdoin, loved to watch the deer eat what my dad fed them. You could get so close to them—within ten feet—and my sons were so excited. They loved to feed the wildlife that frequented my parents' home. They also fed the ducks and turkeys that came by. It was like they were living in a wildlife sanctuary. My sons stayed with me until June 19, 2005. Lucinda got out of jail and drove to Maine with a U-Haul trailer, supposedly to live. Since Lucinda hadn't seen Camden and Bowdoin since the beginning of May, when she was incarcerated, I let the Holleys take the boys with them back to Lewiston so they could see their mother; I was to have them again the next week. Lucinda took my sons and returned to Florida with the U-Haul trailer. The question that remains in my mind to this very day is: Why did she even come to Maine with a trailer?

According to the divorce decree, I was to have my sons for their summer recess from school, and I had believed Lucinda when she said she came to Maine to live. If I had known this was a lie, I would have never ever relinquished the boys. I called her cell phone numerous times to ensure that my sons had arrived back in Florida safely. Lucinda told me nothing but lies. She told me that she was living in her Wiltshire apartment. How could she be living there when she had been evicted?

I did a plethora of research, and I discovered that her boyfriend, Kelly McCane, had bailed her out of jail. I put two and two together and discovered that she was living with him. When I confronted her, Lucinda refused to acknowledge this. In fact, she refused to give me her address, but instead offered a P. O. Box as an address. She attempted to convince me that all my correspondences with her would be forwarded from her old address to this post office box. I *was finally* learning not to take seriously anything that came out of her mouth, but to question everything she said.

Soon after, Lucinda was arrested again for grand theft in Hernando County because of my dismemberment check. She was found guilty and placed on probation for five years. Lucinda couldn't keep her nose clean for long. She was arrested again for shoplifting and writing bad checks. I spoke with her probation officer, Julie Cleveland, and learned that Lucinda had been incarcerated again. She was in jail for violation of probation. Lucinda spent the entire month of November 2005 in jail. Before all this happened, I attempted to contact with my sons, but Lucinda refused to answer her cell phone. I called Kelly McCane's house number, and he answered the phone. I asked to speak with Camden and Bowdoin. Lucinda grabbed the phone, for she had been just released from jail, and in no uncertain terms told me to never call that number again. I replied that I wouldn't have to if she answered her cell phone. She refused to allow me to speak with my sons. Kelly then changed his home phone number to an unlisted number. According to my lawyer, this was another violation of the divorce decree, because I was to have access to my children, wherever they were living.

Before being incarcerated in November 2005, Lucinda rarely let me see my sons. She attempted to use her legal misfortune to support her in this; she said that she couldn't meet me in Pasco County to drop off my sons so they could come with me Hillsborough County, where I lived. I didn't even ask her to meet me where I lived. I offered to go where she lived to pick up my sons, and she adamantly refused. I thought I was doing the fair thing by offering to meet her halfway, in Land O'Lakes, which is in Pasco County. Lucinda said that she could not leave Hernando County because of her probation. I called her probation officer, who told me this was not true. Lucinda could have left Hernando County as long as she informed her probation officer about where she was going and why. To make a long, sad story short, I was rarely allowed to talk to my boys, let alone see them.

If this was the case, why in the hell was I in Florida? Lucinda basically spent the entire month of November 2005 in jail. I attempted to get in touch with Kelly McCane, but he never answered Linda's cell phone. I tried to contact Cassandra, Lucinda's daughter, on her cell phone, but she never answered the phone either. I left numerous messages on both phones, but Kelly never called me back.

Once Lucinda was released from prison for the last time, at the end of November 2005, I got to see Camden and Bowdoin. I took them fishing, and they helped decorate my apartment for Christmas. They both had a blast catching fish and decorating my tree. December 10, 2005, was the last time I got to see my sons or spend any quality time with them. I finished my year at Freedom High School, and once again, my students fared exceptionally well on their exams.

I told Jill in spring 2006 that I planned to resign from my teaching position at Freedom High School. I decided to do this for a myriad of reasons. I finally realized that Lucinda would never follow the divorce decree and let me be a part of my sons' lives. I needed to start living my life for me—not for my students, and not for my kids who I never get to see, but for me. I had so much to learn and do if I was ever to become an independent member of society. Jill didn't believe that I would resign; I guess that she was a little shocked when I did write my resignation letter. The principal, Richard Bartels, was gracious in accepting my resignation, and he wrote me a glowing letter of reference, as did Jill. I thought it would be relatively easy to find a teaching position in Maine. I was wrong.

My Leg

Though I didn't need another reason to leave Freedom High School and Florida, one was quickly given to me. Bloomingdale Woods decided to turn my apartment complex into condominiums. There was no way I could receive a loan to buy a condominium. I told Jill about this, and she was looking for another apartment for me to rent. For me, this was a sign from above and the final nail in the Floridian coffin. Shortly thereafter, I resigned, and my parents once again came to Florida and rented a U-Haul trailer to gather my belongings, which didn't amount to much—a bunch of teaching materials and supplies, some books, clothes, a coffee table, a couple of bookcases, and some fishing equipment. Remember, I didn't get any personal belongings from the divorce ruling. I sold whatever furniture that was given to me, and Jill took back what she had so graciously let me use. Once we packed my meager belongings, we left for Maine. It was time for me to start living for me and not others.

I followed my parents, and we drove straight through to Maine. Mom made a room for me; I was once again living with my parents. I thank God for them every single day, because I don't know where I would be without them. Once I got back to Maine, I saw John Paul Donovan at Atlantic ProCare, and he worked on building me a new socket for my residual limb. I applied for and received MaineCare, which is health care coverage for low-income and disabled people. I thank God that they approved me so I could pay for my prosthetic care and other health care needs; I also had kidney stones, and I had bladder stones. Upon returning to Maine, I had two more surgeries to remove the bladder stones, and I once again had to have a catheter—not that much fun.

After my surgeries, John Paul got me into physical therapy at New England Regional Hospital, where I learned to walk again with my artificial leg. He was upset when he saw me walk when I returned from Florida; I had developed many poor walking habits. Most notably, I hiked my left hip. John Paul and my physical therapists, Shelley Coull and Laura Morgan, were not happy when they saw how I walked. I basically had to start over again and learn how to walk—easier said than done. I had to learn how to once again trust my prosthetic leg, which meant that I had to learn how to spend more time on my artificial side.

I know this sounds complicated, and trust me, it is, but if used correctly, the C-Leg understands my gait. To make my left leg bend, I have to shift my weight from my artificial heel to my toe. Before I started therapy with Shelley and Laura, I couldn't walk appropriately without the use of my cane, which I used on my "real" side.

Shelley and Laura began by testing the strength and range of motion in my residual limb. In order to do this, I had to take off my artificial leg and not be bashful. I had to take off my pants in order to remove my prosthetic leg. As they tested it, they were both impressed with my strength, and they gave me exercises to augment my range of motion and strength. Once they taught me the exercises, I did them religiously; I wanted to get better. They also gave me exercises to do while wearing my leg.

Shelley wanted me to stand on my right side and swing my artificial leg forward and backward. She also wanted me to do the same thing while standing on my artificial side. This was a bit scary for me, but I did it. She made me stand on my real side and swing my artificial leg back and hold it to strengthen my gluteus muscle.

I did all of this, but one day, they scared the hell out of me at therapy—they took my cane away from me. I needed it; I wanted it! Shelley insisted that I didn't need it. I had to walk appropriately without my cane, which meant walking without hiking my left hip. To begin, Shelley had me stand adjacent to a wall, which I could only touch with my left hand. This was not only frightening for me, but also incredibly arduous. Since getting an artificial leg, I always had my cane in my right hand, and now Shelley wanted me not to have anything in my right hand. She wouldn't allow me to touch the wall at all with my right hand. Touching the wall with my left hand forced me to put all my weight on my artificial leg when I walked. While doing this, I had my weight on my left leg long enough to make the artificial knee bend. As I practiced this, the wall was there only as a security blanket for me. This was the first time I walked without my cane. I did this for a couple of weeks in therapy, and then Shelley took the wall away from me, and I had to walk in the middle of the hallway without the cane.

I tried doing this; I could do it, but my form suffered. Shelley and Laura weren't happy, and they were perplexed about why I couldn't do this appropriately without my form suffering. They both came to the conclusion that it was because of the lingering effects of my traumatic brain injury. Shelley consulted my physiatrist, Dr. Elwood Fox, and he agreed. Dr. Fox said I was thinking way too much when I walked. He just wanted me to walk without thinking. I guess I should take this opportunity to discuss all the medications I'm currently taking. Due to my accident and subsequent surgeries, I am on the generic version of Lomitil for diarrhea; I presently take this due the shortening of my colon. My happy pill is the generic version of Celexa. For pain, I use Vicodin. For my brain injury, I am on Baclofen, which, according to the doctor helps me walk better. The doctor argues that without it, I think too much when I walk. He wants me to walk without thinking, which — once again — is easier said than done. I have seen remarkable improvement in my walking and my gait while on the drug. These pills, however, never can begin to replace the relationship that I had with my sons. He told me to walk quickly. Lo and behold — the faster I walked, the better I walked; when I walked fast, I walked without thinking because I was concentrating on moving. I practiced doing this in therapy. Shelley and Laura placed me on a treadmill and observed how I walked. I practiced this for a couple of weeks, and my form on the treadmill improved. Then, I had to graduate from the treadmill to the open floor. This was laborious for me, because on the treadmill I could always hold onto the handles; now, Shelley and Laura wanted me to walk down long hallways with nothing to hold. This was terrifying for me, but I did it. My form had improved; I rarely hiked my left hip, and I was walking on my prosthetic leg. When I saw John Paul, he was pleased with my progress, but I still had a plethora of things to work on to improve my gait. I never realized that walking was so tough.

Back in therapy, Shelley and Laura worked on my walking form. They wanted me to stop dipping on my artificial side when I took a step with my right foot. My father had mentioned this, and he had always maintained that I should lean to the right when I take a step with my prosthetic leg. He was right, but I didn't really do it until my physical therapists told me the same thing. Shelley and Laura tied long, stretchy bands around me and pulled me to the right when I walked with my artificial limb. I practiced walking this way, and I finally realized that my dad was right, and I should have listened to him before. Since the beginning, I could have counted on one hand the number of times I went alone to therapy. My father almost always went to therapy with me so he could learn what I had to do to walk better. He practiced with me all the exercises that my physical therapists wanted me to do. At times, I needed help doing the exercises, and I had to make sure that I was doing them correctly.

Next, Laura taught me to walk along a line with my artificial leg so I could walk with my feet closer together. Evidently, I walked with my feet too far apart, and normal people walk with their feet closer together. There was so much for me to keep in mind when I walked. I never realized that walking properly was so difficult. I wasn't normal, and at this point, I was struggling; I believed that I was walking well enough. To improve, I had to abandon this misconception. For me to do this, I had to be comfortable, which at this point wasn't happening. I had pain in my groin area due to the socket riding too high. I told John Paul about this, and he made some adjustments to my socket and had me wear additional socks over my residual limb, which made my groin area more comfortable. Dr. Fox told me that I hadn't yet realized what the C-Leg could do. I understood it didn't matter what the leg could do; it was much more important that it felt good while I walked. I think that the most vital part of the prosthetic leg isn't the leg itself, but the socket. My residual limb is constantly shrinking, which impacts my fitness and my ability to walk.

I constantly practiced walking with my feet closer together and leaning to my right when I took a step with my prosthetic leg, so that my shoulders wouldn't dip to the left when I walked. My form improved dramatically. Everyone noticed my improvement: Dr. Fox, John Paul, Shelley, and Laura. Laura then set up obstacle courses for me to meander through. As I did this, she focused on my form. Laura wanted me to be able to do this without my walking form suffering. After I practiced this, Laura set up cones for me to pick up, and once I picked up the cones, I had to then learn how to walk backward. If walking forward wasn't hard enough, I now had to walk backwards. In order to pick up the cones, I had to bend down using both my knees and then pick up the cones. Evidently, normal people bend at the knees when they pick things up. Shelley and Laura had grown tired of my argument: "I am not normal."

Their response was, "You have two legs; use them." I practiced this at therapy and at home, and my form and gait dramatically improved. Next, Shelley gave me another exercise to do. She made me do squats, which sound easy to do, but for an AK amputee, this was terrifying and quite strenuous. I did it, though, and I continue to do this exercise occasionally.

Through therapy, my form had improved considerably. Occasionally, I stepped with my real foot rather than having a heel strike. To combat this, Shelley gave me step exercises to do; I would be on my prosthetic limb and take a step with my right foot, ensuring a heel strike. This sounds easy, but it is rather complex. I was once again thinking too much when I walked. Dr. Fox just wanted me to do it without thinking; I think that is why he wanted me to walk quickly and change directions without thinking. According to him, when I did this, my form was much better. Their goal was for me to walk outside of therapy without thinking, and they wanted me to completely abandon the cane. To me, this would have been much easier in flat Florida, but the terrain is much more irregular in Maine. Shelley took me outside and made me walk on irregular ground—up and down, over curbs, and across a busy street. Was she trying to kill me? I always thought that I was a good, respectable patient, so why was she scaring the hell out of me?

For me, the most difficult aspect of this therapy was going down inclines; I had difficulty controlling my speed walking down hills, and it felt like I was always on the verge of falling. It was tough going uphill, too. At first, I wanted to hike my left hip as I was going up, because it was easier for me to do it that way. Shelley made me stay on my left leg long enough to make it bend as I was going uphill. I practiced this for a while, and I am getting better, but going downhill is still terrifying.

Outside of therapy, I applied for a number of teaching positions, but I had no luck landing a position; I am convinced it had nothing to do with my ability to teach social studies and history to students. Rather, it was because I am an amputee. I never lied in my interviews about losing my left leg above the knee. I told my interviewers that I had an artificial leg. To shake things up at an interview I had at Oxford Hills High School, I didn't offer any information regarding my lost limb, and I didn't bring my cane in with me to the interview.

I did exceptionally well, and after the interview, the principal took me on a tour of the building so I could see the classroom I'd have if I were offered the job. I was so excited. I was walking so well, and I was finally confident that I would land a job. The principal told me that I would hear something from him in a couple of days.

During the tour, I came to a flight of stairs. I went up them fine, but unlike a normal person who can go upstairs foot over foot, I am an amputee, and it is impossible for me to go upstairs foot over foot; I can only go downstairs like a normal person. Once the principal saw this, he asked why I was walking so slowly. I told him I have an artificial left leg, and that I am an AK amputee. After climbing the stairs, I went to the classroom and moved around the room fine—through rows of chairs and whatnot. After the interview, I was so excited, because I believed it went so well. I was on cloud nine for the forty-five minute drive home.

I was shocked when I got home and had a message on the answering machine from the principal with whom I had just interviewed. What happened to a couple of days? I called him back, and he told me that I didn't get the job. When I asked him why, he said that I didn't meet his needs. I then asked how I didn't meet his needs, and he refused to answer that question. You can probably imagine the thoughts running around in my head.

Before moving back to Maine, I had successfully taught high school classes in Tampa as an amputee. I firmly believe the only reason that I didn't get that position at Oxford Hills High School is because I am an amputee; it had nothing to do with my ability as a teacher. I can't prove it; this is another reason why this situation is so frustrating. I have applied for many teaching positions.

Finally, a Maine school took a chance on me, and I landed a long-term substitute teaching position at Gorham High School, where I taught American studies classes with an emphasis on English parameters—not history and social studies. I got that position in January of 2007, and I finished that academic year. I continued substituting the following year at Gorham, and the principal there, John Drisko, wrote me a great recommendation. Once I received the long-term substitute teaching position at Gorham High School, my father made me a podium with a shelf in it, and he brought it out to Gorham High School and carried it into my classroom. This was an essential teaching tool for me, because it provided me a base from which I could stand and teach classes. It was also an organizational tool for me; I could organize my lessons for the various classes I taught. One key to being a productive teacher is organization. I also needed to be interactive with my students, and that podium assisted me in doing just that. Thank you, Dad!

The following year, I applied for another long-term substitute teaching gig at Kennebunk High School. The principal there, Nelson Beaudoin, was my principal at Leavitt Area High School, where I had been a teacher before moving to Florida. He gave me that position, which was for a couple of months when the regular teacher left, as he was also a state legislator. I fulfilled that position admirably, and Nelson once again wrote me a glowing recommendation.

I was not in this horrific situation alone. My parents always were right there, supporting me. Of course this was tough on me, but imagine the turmoil my parents were experiencing. What happened to that American dream?

My Parents

For me, that things change is a colossal understatement. The American dream had turned into a nightmare. I woke up with no left leg, no wife, and most tragically, no children. Remember that my ex-wife told my sons that I was dead. I thought I had nothing, but I was wrong; I had two loving and caring parents who would do anything for me.

My father constantly attempted to gain information about me from Lucinda, but she rarely answered the phone, and when she did, he rarely obtained any reliable information. My parents were told I was brain-dead. Her parents were told the same thing. My parents never gave up attempting to gain access to my medical information, but because of the HIPAA laws, medical personnel and later the nursing home staff weren't allowed to furnish any information to my own my mother and father. My parents were going through hell! However, they would not give up.

My parents contacted a neighbor, Heidi Henninger, who was a brain doctor, and she called St. Joseph's Hospital and was able to gain some information regarding the extent of my injuries. To make a long story short, things were not that rosy for me, but at least my parents were now getting the truth. To this very day, my parents—especially my mother—regret not coming to Florida to see me directly after the accident. I don't blame them. There was nothing that they could have done, because I was in a dreadful state, and I probably wouldn't have been able to recognize them or communicate with them; I know that I wouldn't have remembered them. My short-term memory at that point was nonexistent. My Aunt Joyce and Uncle Royce came to see me, and they told my parents what they saw in St. Joseph's Hospital. My brother-in-law, Michael

Loconte, came to see me, and he told my parents that they couldn't handle seeing me in my current state.

I had a huge neck brace, and I had to wear a helmet for numerous reasons—I kept smacking myself in the face and head. There is no way that my mom could have handled seeing me in that condition. I am so thankful that they didn't have to witness that. I was not brain-dead, however, as Lucinda told my parents. Lucinda never told the truth about my medical condition to anyone, and, in fact, she never told my parents or aunt and uncle that I was moved to Heartland Nursing Home. I believe that I was there a week or two before my parents were told where I was, and once again, they couldn't gain any information about me. Whenever they asked for specifics about my medical condition, my parents were told to ask my wife. Whenever they asked Lucinda about my condition, they were told that I was brain-dead and couldn't do anything for myself. Lucinda refused to let my parents have contact with me via telephone while I was con-valescing in the nursing home, so the nursing staff wasn't allowed to let me talk to my parents when they called me.

The staff at Heartland Nursing Home was very nice to me. Initially, I could only call my house to talk with Lucinda and my kids—whenever she decided to answer the phone. In the beginning of my tenure at the nursing home, Lucinda wouldn't even let me talk with my sons.

Through my therapy at the nursing home with Jennifer Cripe, my memory improved, and something miraculous occurred—I remembered my parents' phone number, and I called them.

They were so happy to hear from me. I wasn't brain-dead. I learned from them some of what was going on in the nursing home. I told the staff in no uncertain terms that when my parents called, I wanted to talk to them. I had to sign some papers saying that I, not Lucinda was in charge of my future, and if something were to hap-pen to me, my parents—and not Lucinda—would be in charge of my future, thus eliminating the HIPAA stranglehold over me. All in all, my parents made five trips to Florida to help me, and suffered not only numerous financial expenditures, but also nothing but lies from Lucinda. This continues to have an emotional impact on my parents, especially my mother.

When they came down the final time in May 2006, they brought a U-Haul trailer to gather my belongings. I followed them home to Maine, and hopefully, I will never drive south of the Mason-Dixon Line again. Once I returned to Maine, my parents helped me every day.

For me, the American dream had changed. Of course I still wanted to be happy, which is an integral component of the afore-mentioned American dream, but for me, being happy shifted from being in love with someone and building a life with a significant other to being independent. The dream now consisted of possessing the ability to walk well, independently, without losing my balance. To acquire the ability to walk on irregular ground and to go places without enormous fear were now integral components of the American dream, for me. Public places like stores and other crowded areas alarmed me. In the beginning, my parents would go with me when-ever I went out in public. I would have to take my cane with me and use it to help me in public places. Whether I went to a restaurant or to a store like Wal-Mart, my parents went with me to assist me if I needed help. In the beginning, I used my cane to get into the store, and then I would grab a shopping cart to help me ambulate through the establishment—whether I needed it or not. Whatever purchases I wanted to make were immaterial to me; psychologically, I thought that I needed the cart for balance purposes.

These episodes frightened my parents, especially my mother. With constant therapy through New England Rehabilitation Hos-pital and practice, a weird thing happened. I began to do these types of activities without thinking. I sometimes left the cane in the car; I entered and left establishments without the crutch. Once I real-ized this, I purposely didn't bring the cane with me, and soon after, like a normal person, I only took a carriage if I needed it for items I intended to purchase. Rest assured, this didn't happen overnight, but over time I was becoming independent—new places and doing new things didn't scare the shit out of me anymore. I no longer thought,

I can't do that, I'm an amputee. Instead I began to think I could do it and just had to figure out how.

Many people deserve credit for this remarkable transformation: John Paul Donovan, Dr. Elwood Fox, Shelley Coull, Laura Morgan, and especially my parents. My father had an automatic motorcycle—a 1982 450 Hondamatic, which he gave me to ride and fitted with a suicide shifter so I could shift it with my left hand instead of my left foot. It was an automatic, so I rarely had to shift it anyway. I rode it a couple of times, but my balance wasn't good enough for me to ride it without fear. He bought himself another motorcycle so he could ride with me. I accompanied him to the place he bought his new bike, and they had a kit there so I could turn my motorcycle into a tricycle. It cost a lot of money—over $4,000—but I decided to purchase it so I could ride my bike more comfortably and without fear. Initially, Dad rode with me until he was sure that I could handle it and ride safely.

I rode it well, without fear, and the only things I had to be conscious of were that I didn't have too much ground clearance with the trike, and I had to be aware of soft ground and sand, because the rear wheel would spin. It wasn't a traditional trike, which is driven with the rear two side wheels; instead, it was driven with the middle rear wheel, which is nonexistent on a customary trike. I rode it to physical therapy, and some fellow amputee patients were encouraged when they saw me arrive on my motorcycle. I became sort of an amputee celebrity at therapy; moreover, I was an inspiration to fellow amputees, who wanted to once again ride motorcycles.

I spoke with some fellow patients and told them where I got the trike kit and how it worked. I also rode my motorcycle to my long-term substitute teaching position at Gorham High School. I was a prime example to my students to never give up. The principal there, John Drisko, allowed me to wear shorts when I taught high school classes, for I often had therapy after work in Portland, and it is cumbersome, to say the least, to change pants after teaching. I was required to wear shorts when I went to therapy because the therapists wanted to observe the workings of the artificial knee and my walking gait.

I kept the motorcycle for about a year, and then I decided to sell it. It was important to me to have it and ride it. After the accident, I could have never imagined having the ability to once again ride a motorcycle. I never even dreamed about it. Truth be told, Dad is just as important as my physical therapists; he constantly worked with me and, often anticipating the next step (no pun intended) the therapists would have me do.

I sold the bike for numerous reasons. I never wore a helmet, and this was a huge source of contention for everyone except me. Dr. Fox, John Paul, Shelley, Laura, Mom, and Dad were steadfast against this—according to them—disregard for safety. I didn't care. I had survived the accident, and I wanted to live, and if living meant riding a motorcycle without a helmet and feeling the wind blow through my hair, then so be it. I felt I wasn't alone. God was always with me—on my shoulder, if you will. In short, I didn't like the aggravation of always having to argue with my parents when I rode the bike without wearing a helmet. I guess it began wearing on me that I was disrespecting my parents, who had done so much for me since my accident and continue to do so much for me. It no longer seemed necessary for me to have a motorcycle. I also wanted to once again have a boat; I always believed and continue to believe that time on the water is time well-spent.

I put my trike on the lawn for sale, asking an ungodly price of $5,500. My father also put his new motorcycle beside mine on the lawn for sale, and he was shocked that my bike sold before his—and I received my asking price. I received $5,500 for a 1982 450 Honda-matic, and some people still maintain that there isn't a God? Dad never could sell his bike, and he was only asking a thousand dollars more than me for 2007 700 Yamaha. He later traded it in for a new four-wheeler. His riding days weren't over; he soon bought a scooter, which was extremely beneficial now that gas prices have skyrocketed. Once I sold the trike, I looked for a boat, and Dad and I found an old 1971 Starcraft with a 1988, twenty-horse Evinrude motor and trailer. They wanted a little over $2,000 for it, and he was in the process of moving out west to Colorado. I had $1,000 on me, and I offered it to him for the boat. I had shorts on, and he could see my artificial leg. We haggled, and he said that he would accept $1,200 for the boat, so Dad and I went home so I could acquire the additional $200. We returned so I could buy the boat.

We soon went fishing. Once again, I never thought that I would be able to go fishing again on a boat, let alone be a boat owner again. The boat was good; it was reasonably stable, and the most difficult parts of the boating experience were getting into the boat with my artificial leg and starting the motor. The motor started well, but it often took a few pulls of the rope to start the outboard. It wasn't that hard for me to pull the rope, though it was somewhat painful on my fused right wrist—it was still tolerable. What was intricate in this procedure was my lack of ability to keep my balance. The next year, I invested $400 to convert the outboard to electric start. It is now easy as pie to start.

I can't get my artificial leg wet; it has a computer in the knee, and water would destroy the prosthesis. I told John Paul about my purchase, and he was happy for me, but he was adamant that I couldn't get the C-Leg wet. I purchased from him an archaic leg that wouldn't bend so I could get from the car and trailer to the boat launch and boat. With that leg on, I could walk into the water, which made it easier to get into the boat. I did it this way a few times, but it was cumbersome for me to walk stiff-legged from the vehicle to the boat. To alleviate this situation, I bought some hip waders to wear over my artificial leg, so I could walk regularly. John Paul was and is vehemently against this endeavor; he doesn't want me to make a mistake and fall, ruining the high priced, irreplaceable C-Leg. Thus far, knock on wood, I have been careful and haven't made a mistake. Hopefully, my luck will continue.

As of yet I haven't fished solo on my boat. I have always gone with my Dad or Paul Hodgedon. When I went with Paul, I either fished on his boat or mine, but I needed help getting into and out of the boat so I wouldn't get my left foot or leg wet. They both assisted me in getting on and off of the boat. My Dad thought long and hard about this, and he designed some metal pipes and installed them on both sides of the *Helen Louise,* the name of my boat, which I named after my mother. I use the pipes to assist me getting in and out of the boat. I hold onto the pipe to hold the boat in as I get onboard so the boat won't drift away from me as I hike my artificial leg. I do basically the same thing to get out of the boat.

In the beginning, whenever I became nautical man, I brought my cane with me to assist me in getting onto the boat, but with the pipes, I no longer needed the cane for that. In terms of the American dream, I became independent of the cane, and have been since September 2, 2008. One would think that, under my condition, I would need it in the winter to circumvent snowy and icy conditions, but at this point I am comfortable enough with the leg to walk like a normal person; inclement weather doesn't scare the shit out of me anymore.

Bad weather still scares my parents, but the more I do for myself, the more I help calm their nerves. Physically, as you can probably tell, I rely on my father for assistance. Mentally, I lean on my mom for help. If you remember, I suffered a traumatic brain injury, and I still possess memory problems. My mom helps me deal with this, because, like her father, my mom is very organized. She helps me by writing a plethora of information down for me in an organized fashion so I can quickly put my fingers on it when I need it. She also has organized all my information — my medical files from my numerous surgeries and doctor's appointments, my bankruptcy data, and all the information surrounding the female dog (her arrest records, my divorce decree, and child support records). I often get frustrated if I can't find something or remember something, and she is extremely patient with me. My situation must be exasperating for her, but I would never know it.

Organization is not all that she does. Mom encourages me to have fun. She is saddened that I have to live at home with my parents. I am forever thankful that I have them both in my life. Mom also plays Cribbage and Yahtzee with me, which helps me keep my mind off of my sons, who I never get to see.

In November 2007, Mom took me to an animal shelter so I could pick out a kitty. I picked out a female, buff-colored American short-hair tabby, which I named Sebec after a lake here in Maine that my grandfather used to fish a lot. Sebec is fun for me because, like a child, she relies on me for certain things—food, water, and cleaning her litter box. My parents help me fill these needs, but she also requires attention, and she loves to sit with me and have me pat her; she purrs nonstop. She loves me, and to a certain extent, I am her father. She doesn't replace Camden and Bowdoin, but she helps me deal with the horrific situation my now ex-wife perpetuates. With all that I have had to deal with continue to cope with, most people would question my belief in God. Nothing could be further from the truth.

God

Growing up, and later in high school and college, religion—organized or not—played no role in my life. I never attended any church with my family or any significant other. In brief, I just didn't care about the big questions. That would soon change. In college, I became enamored with Karl Marx and many of his historical and political views regarding the world. If memory serves me right, Marx said that "Religion is the opiate of the people." Since this isn't going to become a political diatribe, suffice it to say that I believe communism would have fared much better if Trotsky and not Stalin had succeeded Lenin. Furthermore, communism wouldn't have the black eye that it possesses today if Lenin had been a better student of Marx and history—but I digress, sorry. Back to God.

In my youth, I wouldn't go have called myself an atheist; I couldn't prove that God didn't exist. I guess if I had to fall under a label, I would have called myself an agnostic. This philosophical religious view would basically accompany me up to my horrendous car accident. Soon after, an awakening and enlightenment occurred for me. If you recall, after the accident, I was in a coma for a number of weeks, and once I came out of it, the doctors reintroduced me back into a coma. They were concerned with brain shearing and brain swelling. I also had to undergo numerous surgeries in an attempt to put me back together. I had my left leg amputated above the knee, and I had roughly half a dozen surgeries on my residual limb due to copious infections. I also had many internal injuries, not the least of which was the shortening of my colon. For approximately six months after the accident, I had a colostomy bag to poop in, and the doctors were unsure whether or not my plumbing would ever be hooked up normally again. Thank God it was; I became preoccupied with that colostomy bag. I always wanted it changed, and I was never taught how to change it myself. It was a messy situation.

One of my first memories upon waking up from the coma was seeing a doctor on his knees at St. Joseph's Hospital, giving thanks to the Almighty for helping him save my life. Lucinda then ridiculed him for saving my life. She said to him something to the effect of, "Look what you have done to his children. He has no leg, a traumatic brain injury, and he will never be the same."

The doctor replied with, "At least he is alive, and he can now be a father to his children." How little he knew about her. Seeing the doctor on his knees praying impacted me immensely. Upon recovering from well over twenty surgeries, my cousin Bonny gave me a Living Bible, which would eventually sway my views regarding religion and God. *The Purpose-Driven Life,* which I would soon read, impacted me also. To date, I have read this book twice, and I agree with the premise that I am not alone. God is with me; I need to give thanks to God for all he has done and continues to do to assist me in my life.

Upon returning to Freedom High School to teach various social studies classes and live with Jill McEwen, with her constant encouragement I began to read the Bible that Bonny had given me in the nursing home. I read it from the beginning, cover to cover. I can't believe how incredibly naive and wrong I was, thinking that "religion is the opiate of the people." My views regarding God and religion have dramatically changed. In fact, I would argue that I have been awakened—literally and figuratively—from the coma, to share this with whomever will listen. I am once again reading the good book cover to cover, and this time I am highlighting important passages, studying them, reflecting upon them, and when in need, asking for guidance from the Almighty to clarify my understanding. Nightly, I say my prayers and give thanks to Him for listening to me and helping me with everything I do and attempt to do.

I have learned that it is not my place to judge Lucinda; a change has taken place within me regarding her, and every pejorative thing that she has done and continues to do to me. I am convinced that she will get what is coming to her for everything that she has done and continues to do. I can already see her writing on the wall. She has remarried a man named Kelly McCane, and she has a domestic violence charge against him. I guess life can't be too great for her. I informed my kids' school and teachers about this circumstance so they could be aware of this situation and keep their eyes open for any evidence of abuse on my sons.

I am basically trying to do everything I can do to protect my children from afar. I rely on God through nightly and daily prayers to protect my children. What else can I do? I can't afford to move back to Florida, and if I did, I have no guarantee that Lucinda would let me be a part of my sons' lives. I am so relieved that I have faith in our savior, Jesus Christ; He comforts me and protects me. God has done so much for me.

He saved me from almost certain death. He protected me through over thirty surgeries, and He has done many little things to assist me. God helped me sell my 1982 motorcycle for the ungodly price of $5,500, and he assisted me in finding that 1971 Starcraft Falcon boat with the 1988 twenty-horse Evinrude motor. I believe that God intervened, having the seller of the craft agree to my $1,200 offer when he was asking a little over $2,000 for the boat. God has been with me every step of the way, pun intended, while I was learning how to walk as an AK amputee. I have faith in God that he wouldn't let me fall, and if I did fall, that he would assist me in getting back up.

My father had a mini stroke that the doctor called a TIA, or transient ischemic attack, while he was shopping with my mother at Lowe's. God intervened to assist my mother in getting my Dad into her vehicle so she could drive him to Maine Medical Center, where he had to stay for three days. Finally, after a barrage of medical tests, he was released, and thus far his health has been fine. For the past couple of months, my mother, with God's guidance, has begun to try to get herself in better shape by walking every day. Thank you, God!

Conclusion

Needless to say, ever since my accident, God has become a vital part of my life and for me, an integral component of the aforementioned American dream. Let's revisit that American dream. Initially, I believed that the American dream was being in love, having children, and raising them with a firm moral foundation—teaching them right from wrong—so they would live that way. It involved owning a home, which is a fundamental piece of Americana. Things have certainly changed. I am no longer married or in love, I no longer am a homeowner, I am no longer a molder and shaper of young minds, and—most profoundly traumatic—I no longer am an integral part of my sons' lives. I have no one but Lucinda to blame for this. It certainly is not from lack of trying.

I constantly attempt to be part of Camden's and Bowdoin's lives. I continually try to call my sons and talk with them, but Lucinda refuses to answer the phone when I call, or even return my messages for my boys to call me. Is it any wonder that I have been prescribed a daily "happy pill" from my primary doctor? As of yet, I have refused to give up, but many people argue that I need to see the writing on the wall. They say that I need to live for me, and one day my sons will seek me out. I hate that I am losing out on being a part of their lives during their growing years. I definitely wanted to be a part of their educational development. Remember that I was a teacher—by all accounts, a damn good one—and I am firmly convinced that I could have been an educational asset for my sons. I know what is needed for instructive achievement at all educational levels, especially the middle and high school levels; I have over fifteen years of teaching experience in those educational settings.

I believe in my heart of hearts that I am a much better role model for my sons than my ex-wife, who has an extensive criminal record. Her oldest child, Cassandra Philbrook, has already fallen into her mother's footsteps. She has been arrested for and convicted of theft at the local Wal-Mart, before even graduating from high school. I guess the old saying is true: "Like mother, like daughter." I learned about this, and about Cassandra's driving violations, from the Hernando County register; all legal violations for adults become part of the public record. Unlike Lucinda's parents, who purposely kept me in the dark about Lucinda's past, I thought that the Holleys should know what is happening to their daughter and to their grandchildren.

Speaking of Lucinda, not much has changed in regards to her legal misfortunes. She has charged her husband, Kelly McCane, with domestic violence. Lucinda never told me about this, but I learned about it from the Hernando County Sheriff's website. I was incredibly shaken up by this—not for Lucinda but for my sons. I had no idea whether or not he was abusing Camden and Bowdoin. I sent all the information I gained from the Hernando County register to my sons' school, Deltona Elementary School, and I implored them to keep an eye out for any signs of abuse—mental or physical. I asked them to keep me constantly updated regarding this and their social and academic progress in school. Camden is in third grade, and Bowdoin is in second.

Once this domestic violence charge was levied against her husband, unbeknownst to me, Lucinda moved with my children and her two other children to a new address. Evidently, she has a new daughter with McCane. Once again, Lucinda clearly ignored the divorce decree, which states in clear English that I am to be immediately made aware of any changes in the living condition and location of my sons.

I periodically check the Hernando County Sheriff's website for any legal violations, but now maybe I should check it daily. I learned that Lucinda McCane is being evicted from 4900 Canonball Court, Spring Hill, Florida. Imagine how shocked I was to discover this; she never informed me that she moved from her previous address, 9683 Balridge Road, which is in total violation of the divorce decree.

Upon learning of this, I immediately contacted the Hernando County Sheriff's Department and spoke with Deputy Lamia, and I informed him that I had no idea where my children were. I gave him all the information that I possessed—her cell phone number and her last known address—and I implored him to find my children.

Shortly thereafter, on May 24, 2009, Lucinda called me and apologized for not telling me that she moved four months ago. This is how I learned about the Canonball Court address. She said nothing about being evicted. I then researched the property and discovered that it was in the process of being foreclosed upon, and that she was renting the property but not paying the rent—hence the eviction notice served on her. When I brought this up, she did what she does best—deny, deny, deny, and if all else fails, deny again. I would like to thank Deputy Lamia for investigating this and forcing her to call me and inform me about where my sons were. I am convinced that Deputy Lamia was with her when she called; her tone had dramatically changed. She sounded genuinely apologetic, and she talked about bringing my boys to Maine this summer to see me. This ruse soon ended a couple of days later, on May 30, when I called to wish Bowdoin a happy eighth birthday. She said that she wouldn't be sending my sons to Maine to see me this summer, which—again—is in total violation of the divorce decree. According to the aforementioned decree, I am to have my sons for six weeks every summer during their summer break from school. Lucinda has blatantly ignored the divorce decree since its inception.

I have spent thousands of dollars taking her back to court on two different occasions, and she basically received a slap on the wrist and promised to follow the divorce decree. This didn't last very long, and then she reverted back to her old ways. I can't afford to continually take her back to court. I guess it is time to listen to my critics and start living my life for me. I will still attempt to reach out to my sons on important occasions, but I will try not to become obsessed with them, because it does no one any good. I know for a fact that Lucinda speaks disparagingly about me in front of my boys; they have both told me this, and it makes them feel badly. After everything I have been through because of this female dog, I have never badmouthed her in front of Camden and Bowdoin. I just wish that she could truthfully say the same thing, but that will never happen.

For me, the American dream has certainly been transformed. I often still dream of being an integral part of my sons' lives and to have them be a part of their grandparents' lives. My parents are elderly, and their health has suffered emotionally and physically from my ordeal. They are hurt by Lucinda's actions toward me and my children. For them, it is now like they have no grandchildren. They are not allowed to speak with them on the phone, send them cards or presents, or see them. This has damaged me on a myriad of different fronts. I feel my parents' pain; in fact, I too live with that same pain. I have to deal with it from my perspective and their perspective, and what about Camden and Bowdoin? Despite the numerous lies that I am sure they are being told about me, I am willing to bet that, at least occasionally, they think about me fondly and miss me. At least, I would like to think so. I miss them and love them so much it hurts.

I need to focus on something else now. Of late, I have focused on my parents and my leg. First things first—my parents mean so much to me. Without them, where would I be? Probably, I would be living on the street somewhere. I have a roof over my head and food in my belly because of them. They are my greatest advocates—my only advocates. I feel so badly for all that I have put them through. I never should have left Maine, and obviously, I never should have married Lucinda. What if I had never gotten married? Or if I had never left Maine? "If" is the biggest word in the study of history. If I had never left Maine, I would be still teaching high school social studies classes, and I would have two legs. Of course, my history would have been dramatically different "if . . ."—but you can't go back.

My artificial limb is on its last leg, pun intended. It makes a noise when I walk, and the socket for my residual limb barely fits anymore. MaineCare refuses to stand behind my C-Leg; in fact, they have yet to pay for it, but according to all the paperwork that I have, MaineCare is supposed to pay for the leg and support it by either ordering me a new leg or repairing the one that I currently have. If the repairs cost more than 60% of the cost of a new limb, MaineCare is supposed to pay for a new leg. I have an upcoming legal hearing to determine the outcome of this mess. Since I have no money, I contacted Pine Tree Legal Assistance to see if they could once again support me in this endeavor with MaineCare. A couple of years ago, I had a legal hearing against MaineCare, and Pine Tree Legal represented me. I won the case, partially because the representative from the state of Maine didn't show up; I won by default. That case was to determine whether or not the state would pay for a computerized electronic artificial limb.

The state of Maine's argument was that MaineCare didn't pay for high-tech devices; they believe that I didn't need one. John Paul Donovan and Dr. Fox's argument was that because of my traumatic brain injury, I did in fact require the C-Leg. Since the state's representative failed to appear at the hearing, I won the case, and the state of Maine was supposed to pay for the leg. I am surmising that because of the dramatic downturn in the economy, the state has failed to live up to outcome of the hearing, and they have yet to pay for the C-Leg. Now the C-Leg is failing—hence the reason for the upcoming hearing. My parents have been with me every step of the way.

It is high time that I do a little something for them. I currently have a part-time job working for Hannaford, a large grocery store. I work fifteen to twenty-five hours per week. Out of that measly weekly check, I pay $87.38 for child support to the state of Florida. There really isn't all that much left over for me, but since I live with my folks, my expenses aren't that extravagant. I give my Mom twenty dollars a week for rent. For the past year, I have attempted to obtain SSI, but the federal government seems to think that I don't warrant SSI; according to them, I make too much money, and I live with my parents. Both of my parents are in their seventies, and we all worry about what's going to happen to me when they're gone.

The United States government didn't care. However, I didn't give up. I switched gears and applied for Social Security Disability

James D. Richardson

Insurance, or SSDI. I had to prove to the federal government that I was disabled. I presumed that being an above-the-knee amputee was more than enough to qualify me as disabled. I sent all my medical information and files to the appropriate agency and waited. I guess that the federal government wasn't satisfied with this plethora of information I forwarded from numerous medical facilities detailing the extent of my trauma; I had to see two more doctors, one for my amputation and my other physical, medical maladies; and the other for my psychological illnesses due to my brain injury. The first doctor reaffirmed all the information I sent to the federal government. Moreover, he said that I hadn't miraculously re-grown my left leg, hence I am still disabled. The second doctor—a psychologist, if you can actually call that a doctor—wasn't as pleasant as the first. I went to see Dr. Margulis at his "office," if you can call his private residence an office. He was not concerned about me, as you will soon see. I had an appointment to see him at 10:15 in the morning. I arrived at his "office," which was in fact his home, in Freeport, Maine. I went with my parents, and thank God that I did. I parked my car in his driveway and sent my father out to the house to ensure that we were at the right place. Dad went in, and sure enough, we were, so I got out of the car to make my way into his house. Dr. Margulis told us to go around front to enter his office. We did as we were told, and I was shocked to see three huge cement slab steps that had no rails to hold onto to enter. Remember—I am an amputee, and yes, while I am walking much better now, it is extremely difficult if not impossible for me to climb stairs without the help of a rail.

Obviously Dr. Margulis was either ignorant of the Americans with Disabilities Act, or he just blatantly refused to adhere to it—I am not sure which. Even though I had my cane with me, there would have been no way I could have entered this office without the assistance of my seventy-year-old father. Once we entered, there was no waiting room for us, and I was told that my car had to be moved because he was expecting a delivery of lumber.

Does this sound like an office to you? That was not all. My parents were told that they could not stay while the doctor met with me.

They were told to drive around for forty-five minutes and then come back to pick me up. At the time of this appointment, gas prices were hovering around four dollars per gallon. I am disabled and unemployed. Once my parents left, I was told that I would meet with the doctor upstairs, in his actual office. How was I supposed to get upstairs? There was no elevator! I had to climb up over thirty narrow stairs. Somehow, I managed to ascend the myriad of stairs to enter his office, which was an upstairs bedroom with a couple of chairs in it. Why couldn't we just sit downstairs? Oh yeah—because lumber was coming to his "office."

Once we sat down, he told me to tell him about myself and explain why I was there. I was wondering myself, but I obliged his inquiry. I told him about my educational background, my fifteen years of teaching experience, and my inability to land a teaching position. I went on to explain my theories about why I had been unable to secure a teaching position—because I am an amputee. I didn't leave anything out. I told him about the Oxford Hills High School scenario.

Dr. Margulis said, "You look upset; you have a ruddy complexion."

Why wouldn't I be red? I just had to climb up over thirty stairs to enter his "office." He told me I have anger management issues. I countered with, "Why wouldn't I be angry? Unlike a normal person, it takes much more energy for me to get around." I told him it wasn't easy for me to enter his "office," and I was upset by his disregard for the ADA and his lack of a waiting room.

He said, "You don't seem disabled," and he asked me why I was applying for SSDI. I was getting a bit angry at the good doctor. I replied that my parents are elderly; they are both in their seventies, and I asked him what would happen to me when they died. He refused to answer that question.

I said, "What am I going to do—be a ward of the state?" I told him that I needed SSDI in order to attempt to become independent of my parents. He possessed all the pertinent information regarding my traumatic brain injury. He asked me how the brain injury impacted my daily living. I responded that I had to be much more anal about everything—specifically that I had to be much more organized in my daily routine, writing everything down so I could remember my appointments, schedule, and bills, He ended the appointment by telling me that I probably wouldn't get SSDI, and that I could appeal that decision.

As I left this appointment, I did have anger management issues. I was irate at this so-called doctor and his total disregard for the Americans with Disabilities Act. Upon arriving home, I penned a letter to Carol Oxley, who is with the Department of Health and Human Services; she was the person who set up this appointment with Dr. Margulis. In that letter, I let her know what had just occurred, in no uncertain terms. A few weeks passed before I heard anything about my application for SSDI. During that period of time, I attempted to get all my ducks in a row. I contacted all of my doctors to let them know what was going on, and they were all very supportive. Most people told me not to get my hopes up, because most people are initially denied benefits and then have to appeal that decision and get a lawyer to help them argue their cases.

I, however, was not most people. I firmly believe that my letter to Ms. Oxley carried a lot of weight, for I had physical evidence and pictures to corroborate my meeting with Dr. Margulis (See appendix B). Eventually, I received a communiqué from the federal government, congratulating me and telling me that I would receive SSDI in the amount of $742 per month. If I comprehend it right, I will continue to receive this monthly allotment if I do not make more than $980 per month at my part-time job at Hannaford. Time will tell if my understanding is accurate.

Once I learned this, I was ecstatic, but my parents' reaction was a bit more tempered. They are pleasantly surprised and thankful about this, but they are under the impression that there will be no way that I can financially survive on my own. They are probably right, both in terms of finances and my mental capabilities—or my lack of mental facilities. My memory still haunts me to this very day. Pine Tree Legal just called me about my upcoming legal hearing against MaineCare. I spoke with Joanne Dobler, and she had numerous questions about my accident and finances at the time of the accident; I struggled to answer her inquiries. I just can't remember! I rely on my parents, especially my mother, to assist me with this data. Whatever I know about the accident and the time surrounding the event I get from my mom. I just can't remember.

What has happened to that American dream? For me, the American dream now means for me to become an asset—no longer a burden—to my parents. In whatever time they have left on this planet, before they join God in heaven, I want them to feel that I will be able to survive on my own. I am attempting to become more self-sufficient by obtaining the medicines and whatnot on my own rather than relying on my parents to get them for me. I am also trying to be more proactive in my relations with Atlantic ProCare and Pine Tree Legal. Before, my parents dealt with these situations themselves. In brief, I want my parents to be happy, because God knows they have been through enough.

Initially, I brought my father fishing with me because I couldn't get on or off the boat by myself; I needed his help. Once on board, I realized that Dad enjoyed fishing almost as much as I did. I always told him that time on the water was time well-spent, and he was beginning to see the light. Dad and I are fishing opposites; he is a bait man, while I am a fly man. Initially, I was the only one catching fish. I taught him how to sew on smelts, and he began to get some hits. One day, we were fishing a local, small lake named Crystal Lake, and Dad was using worms; I was trolling a streamer fly, and something miraculous happened—Dad caught a huge rainbow trout. After this, it became crystal clear that Dad was hooked on fishing. He even sometimes goes fishing by himself to the local river, and he has good luck. He finds it relaxing and fun. This makes me so proud. I just wish that I could give this feeling to my sons.

Because of my Dad's mini stroke, he needs to relax. I just hope that I can assist my mother in calming down as I have with my dad.

After reading this, you can probably tell that my mother and I are very close; we always have been and always will be. I am not sure whether this is an asset or burden for her. I know that she feels my pain and basically has to deal with it as I have to deal with it. To try to help my Mom, Dad convinced her to purchase an old convertible—a 1993 Geo Metro. Mom loves it, and I like to go riding with her in her two-seater. She likes that I want to go with her wherever she goes. I truly believe that this brings her pleasure, which is what I want. I desire for Mom to take better care of herself by exercising more and being more proactive in her health. At times, I threaten to call the doctor for her if she won't do it, and on a couple of occasions, I have called the doctor on her behalf. In short, I just want my parents to be healthy and happy and to not worry about me. If I could accomplish this, I would be over halfway to living my new American dream.

What is the other half? I want to become fully independent. Is it possible? Can I survive on my own? I hope it is a long time before I ever have to find out, but it is better to be safe than sorry. I hate to think what my life would be like without my parents, but I have to. I need to be able to function alone. I want to be able to go on my boat and fish alone. To do this, I need to learn how to both launch and retrieve my boat to the trailer without getting my leg wet. I also want to be able to go golfing alone—to be able to swing a golf club and hit the ball, hopefully straight and far, without falling down. This is asking a lot, I know. To attempt to do this, I need to improve my balance.

I also need and want to have the ability to take care of our ancient homestead. This requires the capacity to maintain the grounds in all seasons. I know that it probably won't look as nice as it currently does, with Dad taking care of the grounds, but I want it to look pleasant. I believe that I can mow the lawn and trim weeds where I have to, but I am unsure about whether or not I can paint the house when needed or fix things when necessary. Dad is very good at fixing things when they break. He is also very astute in preventive maintenance. I hope and pray that I can be half the man he is in this regard. I am convinced that he has saved himself copious headaches and dollars by being so anal about maintenance. Before my tragic accident, I always maintained my own vehicle, and I was also quite anal about it. Writing everything down in a maintenance log ensured that I wouldn't miss a scheduled oil change or whatever. Whenever I sold a vehicle, the buyers were impressed by this, and I think that it helped me get my asking price.

I still maintain a maintenance log, but as of yet I haven't changed my own oil and filter solo. As an amputee, it is incredibly complicated for me to get on the ground and maneuver around under my car. It is difficult, but not impossible, and I think I can do it. In the winter, I will need to clean the driveway of snow, and I think that I will be able to run the snow blower and Dad's four-wheeler with a plow attached to it. I will have to try it this upcoming winter to see if I can do it. If I am successful in all of this, I am well on my way to being independent and, thus, living my newfound American dream.

This is all dependent on me having an artificial leg that will allow me to stand and walk on two legs. Anything extra would be just icing on the cake, but the frosting has always been my favorite part of any cake. I never even thought of or considered my sons being the equivalent to the tasty stuff on a pastry, but to me, Camden and Bowdoin are the icing on the cake. I hope and pray that one day they will seek me out, and I will be able to prove to them that their Dad never forgot about them and always tried to be an essential part of their lives. At this point, this is all in God's hands, and I hope and pray that He won't let me down. God bless you, Mom, Dad, Camden, and Bowdoin!

James D. Richardson

Appendices

Appendix A
Diary for My Sons

8/11/05: I called Camden and Bowdoin, and Bowdoin didn't want to talk with me, and Camden said hi, but both said in the background that they didn't want to see Daddy. They both had told me in the past that this is what Mommy tells them all the time. I didn't get to see my children this weekend. This was my weekend to have you, but your mother refused.

8/13/05: I went swimming today, and I thought of both of you, Camden and Bowdoin. I wish you could have been here and played with Daddy. I love you and miss you both.

8/21/05: I went bowling last night with Lisa and Jessie. Wish you could have been there. It was fun, and I did well—I didn't even fall. I thought about you all evening, and I told everyone about both of you and showed your pictures. I love you and miss you so much.

8/25/05: I called to speak with you both and make arrangements for you to see Daddy tomorrow until Sunday, but your mother would not make plans. It is my weekend to see you and be with you. I miss you and love you so much. I haven't seen you for almost a month. Lucinda finally told me your teacher's name — Mrs. Leonard.

9/01/05: Your teacher called me, Camden, and told me that you are doing well. I am so proud of you and wish I could talk with you and see you and Bowdoin.

9/04/05: I called today to speak with both of you, but your mother wouldn't answer her cell phone, and since I don't have your house phone number, I couldn't speak with you. Your mother's boyfriend changed the number on July 24 to an unlisted number, and your mother refuses to give it to me. I have been worried about you this past week. I hope you were all right this week and your mom was nice to you. Your mom had to go to court on Friday, 9/2/05, where she pleaded guilty to grand theft. She received five years of probation. I went swimming today, and for the past two weeks, people at my apartment pool complex asked about where you were. You are loved and missed by many people. I wanted to ask how school is for both of you. Your Daddy knows, Bowdoin, that you started school on Monday, and I tried to talk with you, but your mother refused. I miss you and love you both tremendously.

9/09/05: I tried to pick you both up so I could see you and celebrate your birthday, Camden, but your mother refused to meet me in Land O'Lakes; she claimed that she couldn't leave Hernando County, so I drove to your house, but your mother refused to answer the door. I bought you a cake, Camden, which will spoil before you even get to see it. I have many presents for your birthday, Camden, and I have a couple for you too, Bowdoin. I have been thinking of you both lately, and I miss and love you both very much. Daddy has to go to a specialist for his arm, and I may need surgery. I wish that I could see you and talk with you. It was my weekend to be with both of you, but once again, your mother refused to follow the divorce decree.

9/17/05: I am thinking of you both right now — especially you, Camden, because it is your birthday. I have presents for you, but your mother won't let me see you. I miss you and love you both. Happy sixth birthday, Camden! I called today, and you hurt me when you said that you don't want my gifts.

9/22/05: I talked with both of you tonight, and you were both happy to hear from Daddy, and you can't wait to see me. You were very excited about going to Chuck E. Cheese with Dad. I can't wait to see you and be with you and to celebrate your birthday, Camden. Lucinda argued that you both didn't want to be with me, but you both said that you can't wait to be with Dad.

9/25/05: I got to have and see you this weekend. I picked you up yesterday at 11:20. Lucinda was twenty minutes late. I had to drive to Brooksville because Lucinda didn't get permission to leave Hernando County. I gave you some presents, and you both enjoyed them: videos, a shirt, and a necklace for your birthday, Camden, and a video and game for Bowdoin. Both of you told me that Lucinda received a diamond ring and is going to marry Kelly. I had to bring you back today at noon, so I only had you for 25 hours, so we couldn't do too much. I wanted to go to Chuck E. Cheese and the park, but we didn't have enough time. You both wanted to go, but Lucinda wouldn't let you stay any longer.

9/27/05: I called your school today, Bowdoin, but your mother lied to me about where you were going to Head Start. I called your mother, but she wouldn't answer me when I asked for your school's name and phone number. She said she was at the doctor's office with you, Camden. She did not call back to inform me as to how you are or when your surgery is. I am so worried about you both, and I think of you and love you and miss you both tremendously.

10/02/05: I have been thinking of you both every day. It is approaching the two-year anniversary of my accident. You never knew this, but a couple of weeks before my accident, your mother lied to everyone, saying that she had cancer again and couldn't be around you because she was getting radiation treatment. She also said she was staying at the Catholic Church. All of that was a lie. Roxanne from the church called me to tell me that she was not staying at the church. As it turns out, she never had a cancer treatment—she didn't have cancer. She was with her boyfriend, a guy named Lonny. We didn't know anything about this. Mimi and Papa came down to watch you while Daddy worked. They both received calls from men who wanted to know if Lucinda was married.

Your mother cheated on me before the accident. You'll understand someday when you have a relationship with a girl, that you want and expect her to be faithful. Your mother was never faithful to me, and it hurt so much because it hurts both of you as well as me. Once I found out that Lucinda was not getting cancer treatment, she forced me to leave our house. I never should have left. A week later I had the car accident. She was with this Lonny guy from 2003 through the spring of 2004, but he found out what a liar Lucinda is; she told him that she needed thousands of dollars to have a funeral and to bury her mother, who wasn't even dead. He called the Holleys and discovered this. He then broke up with her. I have no respect for this Lonny guy, because he knew she was married and had a family when he got involved with her.

After Lonny, Lucinda got involved with a guy named Joe Kelly. He worked for Executive Curbing. This relationship didn't last that long. Both of these relationships I didn't know too much about because I was in a nursing home. I figured it all out when Billy Fagan and his wife Jasmine brought you both out to Heartland Nursing Home to see me because they were told that I was dead, as were both of you, by Lucinda. You see, Lucinda and I were still married, and she was committing adultery. You two were so happy to see me, and Camden, you said, "I told you, Bowdoin, that Daddy is not dead." You both hugged me so much and cried; you were both so happy to see me.

Lucinda's current man, Kelly Joseph McCane, spends all kinds of money on her, taking her to Mardi Gras and the Daytona 500. I have no idea who was watching both of you while Lucinda was away partying and drinking for weeks at a time. Your mother has a drinking problem, a problem being faithful, and many legal problems. I'll provide you with copies of her extensive arrest record.

10/08/05: I am supposed to have you this weekend, but your mother refused to make arrangements for me to pick you up, let alone see you. I miss you and love you both.

10/09/05: I am supposed to be with you, and I miss you both so much. Your mother won't let me know anything about your health. I know that you are supposed to have your tonsils out soon, Camden, but your mother won't tell me the date or time. I haven't been allowed to talk with you for over two weeks. I miss you and am thinking of you too, Bowdoin. I fed the ducks today, and I told them all about you both. The ducks miss you guys.

10/16/05: I called to speak with you both today, and Cassandra answered the phone and said that you were home, and that Lucinda has a new cell phone, and this number was now hers, and that she has moved to Florida. I have no way of getting in touch with you; Cassandra refused to give me the number to the house or Lucinda's new cell phone. I wanted to see how you guys were and to tell you about Daddy's surgery this week. I love and miss you both a lot, a lot, a lot! I have presents for you both to open if and when I ever get to see you. Love, Daddy.

10/20/05: I just learned that your mother was arrested 10/10/05 and 10/14/05 for shoplifting and some other crime. I am worried about you and love you. I have surgery today, and your mother wouldn't let me talk with you. I hope I'll be all right, and I'll try to talk with you after my procedure.

10/29/05: I called to talk with you, but your mother wouldn't answer the phone or return my call or message. Daddy wanted to tell you about his surgery and wish you a happy Halloween. I hope you have a good Halloween. I miss and love you both.

11/01/05: Arthur just called. Lucinda was arrested again for something—perhaps not paying her fine, according to Cassandra. Her probation officer called Arthur to let him know.

11/02/05: I called Julie Cleveland (Lucinda's probation officer) today, and Lucinda was arrested for a violation of her probation. Arthur called tonight, and Lucinda is still in jail and may be until November 29. She sold her Land Rover and hired an attorney.

11/04/05: I called to talk with you tonight, and Kelly allowed me to say hi to you both. Then, Cassandra got on the phone, and I asked her when I could see you, but she refused to answer, so I asked to speak with Kelly, and once again Cassandra refused. I can't talk with your mother because she is in jail and has been since 11/01/05 for shoplifting and violation of her probation. I am worried about you, and I miss you so much. I am saying my prayers for you both numerous times every day. I love you both very much.

11/09/05: I called to speak with you both on Lucinda's cell phone at 4:45 p.m. and Cassandra cell phone 45 minutes later, but no one returned my call. I want to see you and visit with you. Lucinda is still in jail. I haven't forgotten about you, and I miss you so much. I am so worried about you. I love and miss you both so much. This is very hard on me. When I called on the fourth of November, I asked to speak again with Kelly about having you both for Veterans Day weekend, but Cassandra wouldn't put him on the phone again. I haven't seen you since September 25, and if I had it my way I would see you every other weekend because your Dad follows the law. In fact, I would have you all the time. I am so worried about you both with Thanksgiving coming up and your mother still in jail. You should be with your Dad. I am trying everything in my power to get you.

11/11/05: I called both Lucinda cell phone and Cassandra at 10:30 a.m. today, Veterans Day, to talk with you and inquire about getting you this weekend, but no one returned my call. I love and miss you both tremendously.

11/13/05: I was supposed to have you this weekend, but Kelly wouldn't arrange it. I bought all kinds of duck food so you could both feed the ducks. I am thinking of you, and I love you both very much.

11/18/05: I called both Lucinda's and Cassandra cell phones to speak with you so you could wish Daddy a happy birthday. I haven't seen you or talked with you on my birthday for three years. I love you and miss you both! I haven't seen you since September. I want to see you every day, or at least every other weekend, but Lucinda and her boyfriend won't live up to the divorce decree.

11/20/05: I didn't give up, and tried again twice today, but no one would answer the phones or call me back. I miss you guys so much. Daddy loves you.

11/28/05: I have been so worried about you both! Your mother has been in jail since November 1, and you have been under the care of your mother's boyfriend. I have tried to talk with him, but Cassandra refused to let me speak with him so I could find out if you were both all right. I called your mother's cell phone and Cassandra's cell phone and left numerous messages telling you that I loved you both and missed you, but rarely did anyone call me back. I missed you over Thanksgiving, and I was very worried about you. I think of you both numerous times every day, and I love you!

12/10/05: I finally got to have you today and tomorrow. I took you both fishing, and we caught large bass, and you had fun. You both decorated the Christmas tree and made Christmas decorations. Bowdoin did an excellent job decorating the tree. Camden said that he had a blast playing at McDonald's. You both enjoyed opening your Christmas gifts. I totally enjoyed our time together, and I can't wait to see you again.

12/25/05: I thought about you both today very much. I hope you had a great Christmas. I tried calling you, but Lucinda wouldn't answer the phone, but remember that Daddy loves you both very much. I am supposed to have you for a week over Christmas break, but Lucinda doesn't follow the divorce decree. We would have had so much fun. I am constantly thinking about you both.

1/1/06: I called to wish you a Happy New Year and to talk with you, but Lucinda wouldn't answer the phone or return my message. I am thinking of you guys, and I wish we could see each other to go fishing and play air hockey. Daddy loves you both so much!

1/7/06: I made some pictures of both of you, and I look at them constantly. I have called you numerous times from Christmas up to today, but Lucinda wouldn't answer her phone. I hope that you have gotten to at least listen to all the messages that I left for you. A moment doesn't go by that I am not thinking about you. Daddy loves you both so much! I miss you both so much! I got a frame for your school picture, Camden, and it looks great. I wish I had a school picture of you, Bowdoin, but your mother wouldn't give me one.

1/8/06: Lucinda finally called back last night at 7:00, and I was allowed to speak with both of you for literally two minutes, and you both told me that you got a new puppy for Christmas. I know you will take great care of it and teach it all kinds of new tricks. You're both the puppy's Dad—raise it well. I know you will. I love you and miss you both very much. I haven't seen you guys for a month. I was supposed to have you for a week over Christmas break, but your mother refused. She doesn't follow the divorce decree.

1/15/06: I miss you guys so much! I haven't seen you once in 2006. I am so sad! I want so much to see you and be with you, but your mother refuses to let you see me. I have a long weekend this weekend, as you do from school (Martin Luther King Day). It would have been nice to get together and see each other, but your mother refused. It appears as if she won't let us see one another, but never forget that your Dad loves you both so much, and I am constantly thinking of both of you.

1/21/06: I am thinking of you both so much. Do you remember all the fun we used to have when we lived at house on Sagamore Street? We use to play tackle every day. We used to do the Slip 'n Slide, play in the pool, play catch, and you used to help Dad do all the yardwork. We had so much fun! I used to play with you in your rooms, with all your toys, and often we even slept together when we were so tired from playing so hard. I am so sorry that your mother lost our house. We used to go fishing two to three times a week and we all caught fish—crappies, sunfish, and bass. You both loved fishing with Dad so much. I loved it, too. I am sorry that your mother sold all of my and your fishing gear. She had no right.

1/27/06: I hope you both are happy and healthy. I haven't seen you since December 10, 2005. I haven't spoken with either one of you since January 8, 2006. I miss talking with you and finding out about you. I hope school is going well, and I miss you and love you both so much.

2/6/06: I called yesterday to speak with both of you, but Lucinda wouldn't answer the phone or return my message for you. I got a picture of all three of us from Lisa, and it is very nice. I can't wait for you both to see it. I wish your mother would send me some pictures of you both. I still haven't received your school picture, Bowdoin. I don't know why your mother is so mean to me. I still haven't seen you in 2006. I miss and love you both very much.

2/12/06: I called yesterday to talk with you, Camden and Bowdoin, but Lucinda wouldn't answer the phone. I left a message for you, but I'm sure you never got it. I wish I had your land line phone number so I could call and actually get the chance to talk with you. I miss you both and love you both very much.

2/19/06: I called you guys yesterday, but Lucinda didn't answer the phone. I left a message telling you both that Daddy loves and misses you every minute of every day! I haven't seen you since December 10, 2005! I still have your Christmas stockings to give you. I don't know why your mother is so mean to not let us spend time together or even talk with each other. I say my prayers every night, praying for your happiness and good health. I am reading the Bible and searching for answers and guidance. I love you, Camden and Bowdoin, and I miss you both very much.

3/4/06: I still haven't been allowed to talk with you or see you. Lucinda refuses to let me have any contact with you. She is mad because she knows that you both miss me and love me. Daddy does have some good news for you. I can now go up and down stairs. I no longer have to use an elevator. I have been working so hard physically. I can't wait for you both to see me and what I can now do. I am working too hard for both of you. I want you to be proud of your Dad. I know Lucinda tells you all kinds of bad stuff about your Dad. All lies! Your Dad is so proud of you, Camden and Bowdoin. I miss you and love you both with all my heart and brain. I called today at 4:15 p.m., and Lucinda wouldn't answer the phone, so I left a message. Hope you get my messages, but I doubt it! I'm sure Lucinda tells you both lies, like "Daddy never calls you, and he doesn't love you." All lies! It is so hard for me not to talk with you and not to be with you.

3/12/06: I called yesterday and left a message for you guys to call me, but I bet you didn't even get the message. I went swimming for the first time since my wrist/arm surgery in October last weekend. I wish you guys could have been here with me to swim. I watched Scooby Doo today and thought of you both. I have some Scooby slippers for you, Bowdoin in your Christmas stocking; I hope that you will get them while they still fit. I love you Camden James, and I love you, Bowdoin John. You are my sons, and regardless of what Lucinda says and does, she can never change that! I just wish that we could see each other and talk with one another at least once every two weeks. I haven't seen you since December 10, 2005, and I haven't talked with you on the phone since January 8, 2006. If I had it my way, guys, I would always be with you!

3/18/06: I am supposed to have you both this week for spring break! A whole week with your Dad—we would have so much fun, but your mother will never answer the phone when I call, and she will never return any of my messages. Please know that a day does not go by that I don't think of you and wish that I could talk with you and be with you. I am so sorry that your mother broke our family up. I hope that one day you will see what happened and understand that your Dad has always and will always love you and support you. I say my prayers every night, praying to God to look out for you and to keep you safe and happy. I also pray that you think of me with good thoughts. I know that your mom has tried to poison your minds against me, and for that I am truly sorry, and I also pray that she will stop that. I hope that God will forgive her for her actions. Camden and Bowdoin, I love you and miss you so much.

3/23/06: I just went in to sign papers declaring bankruptcy. When I was hurt in the car accident, Lucinda never paid any of the bills, but they were all in my name. I didn't know that Lucinda wasn't paying any bills; I was stuck in the nursing home and hospitals. She took out plenty of credit cards in my name and never paid for them, so my credit was devastated. She also had her car repossessed, but once again, it was in my name, so her credit wasn't affected, but mine was destroyed. The lesson to learn from this, sons, is to never only put your name on any loans or credit cards; at least have your significant other's name too, so you won't be solely responsible. She also forged my name on my dismemberment check for $17,000 and bought herself a Land Rover. That money was supposed to go for an artificial leg for me. She never wanted me to get a leg or get better; she never wanted me to ever come home again, for that would ruin her affairs and her sleeping around and her drinking. There is so much I can and will tell you when you are ready. I just pray and hope that you are both being treated well and are safe and happy. Your Dad thinks about you both every day! I miss and love you both so much. I hope that we can see each other or at least talk with one another soon.

3/25/06: I called to speak with you both today, but your mother wouldn't answer the phone. I left a message, but no one returned my call. I am so mad and sad at your mother for not letting me talk with you and see you. A day never goes by without me thinking of you both. I know it isn't your fault.

4/8/06: I have been watching Boston Red Sox baseball games lately, and I have been thinking of both of you. Do you remember when Daddy used to coach you in both basketball and baseball? I loved coaching you both. I am getting around better now; I am not even using the elevator. I am going up and down stairs now. I wish your mother would let me see you so I could show how much you Dad has improved, but she will never answer the phone or return my messages to you guys. Please remember that your Dad misses you and loves you both so very much. I wish I could hear your voices right now!

4/14/06: It is Good Friday—Easter weekend! Do you remember hunting for eggs and Easter candy? Daddy had a hard time trying to find just the right place to hide all your eggs and candy. It was difficult for Dad to remember every place that he hid all the treats, but sure enough you guys found everything. That was so much fun for all of us. I certainly hope and pray that you have a fine Easter. I am constantly thinking of you both, Camden and Bowdoin. It is so hard not to be with you during the holidays; moreover, it is really difficult not to be with you every day or at least talk with you on the phone, but your mother will never return my calls. I don't blame you guys at all. Daddy loves you and thinks of you every day!

4/24/06: I can't believe that your mother will never answer my calls so I can speak with you; moreover, I can't believe that I still haven't seen you in this New Year. I haven't seen you since December 10, 2005. Why do I even try? The answer is that I love you both so much, and come hell or high water, I will never stop trying to a part of your lives. I hope that one day you will know that your Dad has never or will never give up trying to be a part of your lives. Daddy loves and misses you both so much!

5/14/06: I love you, Camden and Bowdoin. I can't believe that I haven't seen you at all in 2006. I have no idea why your mother won't return my calls or let you guys see your Dad. I have not forgotten about you, and I never will. The ducks come by every day to see you, Bowdoin and Camden, so you can feed them. I still have Christmas presents for you guys to open. I love and miss you so much! I cry just thinking about it and about you, because it hurts so much not being able to see you and talk with you. I have no idea why your mother is so mean.

5/21/06: I went swimming today, and I wish you could have been with me to play at the pool with all the kids. Jessie and Lisa came over yesterday and fed the ducks; I remember how you both loved to feed the ducks. I am constantly thinking about you both, Camden and Bowdoin, and Daddy misses you and loves you both. I sent two birthday cards to you, Bowdoin; I hope you got them. I have called, but your mother won't answer the phone or return my messages.

5/27/06: I called today to talk with you, but your mother said that she wasn't home so I couldn't speak with you, Bowdoin and Camden. I asked to have the house number, but she refused, so I can't talk with you. I miss you and love you and worry about you both very much.

5/30/06: I called to wish you a happy birthday, Bowdoin, but your mother wouldn't answer the phone so I left a message for you. Hope that you got it.

6/9/06: I am supposed to have you and be with you this summer, but your mother refuses to live up to the divorce decree. I miss you and love you both very much! I see the deer and feed them every day. I think of you both and say my prayers every night for both of you.

6/17/06: I have been thinking of you both a lot lately. Bowdoin, I doubt very much if you will even remember your Dad. This makes me very sad; I cry when I think about it very much. Camden, I think that you can at least remember me, but I doubt that you remember all the fun things that we used to do. I know that your mother does nothing for you to foster a relationship with me. In fact, I believe she just talks badly about me in front of you both. For this, I am sorry, but rest assured that none of it is true. I love you and miss you both so very much.

6/25/06: I bought a motorcycle and am now riding it. I wish you could see it, and I could give you both a ride. I see the deer every day and feed them. I wish you could see them, Bowdoin, because you always love seeing and feeding the deer. I miss you, Camden and Bowdoin, and I love you both very much. I call you both, but your mother never tells you so you can't call me back. For this I am truly sorry.

6/29/06: Camden, I hope everything went well in school this past year. Your mother never told me how you were doing or kept me abreast of your progress or accomplishments. I also hope that school went well for you, too, Bowdoin, and once again your mother never informed about your progress or accomplishments. I feel like a stranger! This is what your mother wants. I want to be in your lives and a part of your lives, but your mother, for some insane reason, won't let me. I don't even know what sports you are into. Always remember that your Dad loves and misses you!

7/1/06: I really hope you guys have a safe and fun Fourth of July weekend. I remember when we lived in our house in Turner, Maine, we went to the parade, had cookouts with Sydney and Avery and their families, and had sparklers. We also had an outside fire to roast marshmallows and watch the fireworks. We would set up a tent to sleep outside and do some backyard camping. It was so fun! Sydney and Avery always ask about both of you. Your mother stole from Sydney's and Avery's parents and sold their stuff in a garage sale, and that is why Lucinda doesn't have any contact with Melody and Aaron, who are Sydney's and Avery's parents. I could and will tell you more about this later. Your Dad loves and misses you so much, Bowdoin and Camden. I call at least once a week, but your mother refuses to let me talk with you. Most often, she refuses to answer the phone, so I leave a message, but your mother never returns the call. I bet that she never tells you that I called and left a message for you. This hurts me so much, Camden and Bowdoin. I cry just thinking about it. I know that your mother tells you hurtful things about me and lies to make me look bad in your eyes. These are all lies, and I can and will prove it to you someday—hopefully soon.

7/2/06: I saw a father walking with his son today down the sidewalk, telling his son to avoid the puddle, and it reminded me of both of you. Your mother has stolen so much from me! Not to say anything about all my possessions, which I could list—and will someday tell you everything and all the items that she stole—but what I am thinking about now is all the time she stole from me: time from you both, the time and experiences of being your Dad. This makes me so sad and very mad. How can she be so mean? Remember that Dad loves you both very much and misses you so much, Camden and Bowdoin!

7/12/06: I hope you guys remember Mimi and Papa. They bought numerous Christmas presents over the past couple of years for you both and sent them down to you, but your mother refused to let you have them. In fact, she sent them back to Mimi and Papa unopened. Aunt Julie and Nicole have sent you both gifts, too, and once again Lucinda sent them back unopened so you never were allowed to receive anything from your family on my side. This hurt Mimi and Papa very much as well as Aunt Julie and your cousin Nicole. They all love you and want the best for you! This also hurt me very much. I don't know why your mother is so hurtful. Does your mother ever let you call your grandparents, Mimi and Papa? I know she doesn't let you have any contact with my side of the family. I am so sad and mad about this because it hurts both of you so much. We all love you, Camden and Bowdoin, so much.

7/20/06: I spoke with and visited Sydney and Avery, your friends, yesterday. Remember that they were your friends who lived in Maine and Florida. Marissa was Cassandra's friend and the Taylors were my friends and your mother's. I am still friends with Sydney's and Avery's parents, but your mother is not because she stole from them and sold some of their possessions without their knowledge or permission. This all happened after my car accident. You both stayed with the Taylors after my accident because your mother told them that she was too busy visiting me in St. Joseph's Hospital. This was a lie! She was staying with her boyfriend at the time—a guy named Lonny. She was married to me but having an affair. Sydney and Avery asked all about you, but I couldn't tell them much because I haven't been allowed to speak with you since January, and I haven't seen you since December 2005. It was nice for me to see your friends and the Taylors. I went swimming with them, and they were all very sad that you guys haven't seen me as I am as well. I love you and miss you very much, and I think about you both, Bowdoin and Camden, every day. In fact, I think about you numerous times every day.

8/8/06: I have called you both numerous times, and no one answers the phone, so I left messages, but no one returns my calls. I am worried about you guys so much. I know school has started again, and I have no idea who your teachers are or if they even know that I exist. I hope your mother has placed my information on your school records. I doubt it; but I do hope that she did. I should receive all your grades and attendance records. I sure hope that I do.

8/23/06: I miss you guys so much, and I think about you every day. Remember that your Dad loves you so much! I don't know why your mother won't give me the phone number of where you are living; she is so mean!

9/1/06: I called today to talk with you both and tell you about my surgery that I had today, but your mother refused to answer the phone, so I left a message for you but no one returned my call.

9/2/06: I called today to talk with you, my sons, but your mother refused to answer the phone. I also called Cassandra's cell phone, but once again, no answered the phone, so I left messages on both cell phones for you; no one returned my call.

9/6/06: Camden and Bowdoin, I feel so all alone not being able to talk with you or see you. I want to hear about your days at school and wait for you to get off the bus and play with you and help you study and do your homework. Your mother doesn't tell me anything that is going on in your lives. I never wanted to leave you, but your mother couldn't keep her pants on! Not a day goes by without the both of you in my thoughts and prayers. I love and miss you guys so much that it hurts!

9/11/06: This is the fifth anniversary of 9/11—the most severe catastrophe to hit the United States in the history of this country. Your birthday is coming up, Camden, and I really hope that I get to talk with you on your birthday. Bowdoin, I tried to talk with you on your birthday, but your mother refused to allow me to speak with you. I love you both so much, and I miss you.

9/15/06: I called today at 4:00 p.m. to talk with you, Camden, and to wish you a happy birthday, but your mother wouldn't answer the phone. Her boyfriend Kelly answered, and I asked him to speak with you, but he refused. This makes me so mad. I will try to call again in a couple of days.

9/16/06: I called today at 12:15 p.m. to wish you happy birthday and to see if you got my cards and pictures. Lucinda refused to answer the phone, so I left a message for you and Bowdoin telling you that I missed you and loved you. I have presents for you, Camden, for your birthday; if I ever get to see you, I will give them to you. I also have birthday presents for you, Bowdoin. I never got to talk with you on your birthday. I don't know why your mother is so mean!

9/18/06: I called your school today, Camden and Bowdoin, and I found out your teachers' names. Mrs. Webber said that you're doing well, Bowdoin, in school and you're in speech therapy and improving. Mrs. Cramer is your teacher, Camden, and she said that you are doing well. Both teachers are supposed to keep me informed about your grades and attendance records. I told them both that your mother was incarcerated last year for the entire month of November. I miss you both and am so proud of you both. I called again yesterday to wish you a happy birthday, Camden, but your mother refused to answer the phone or return my calls. I just found out that you were both in Maine this summer, and the Holleys never let us know that you were both in Maine so you couldn't see me or talk with me.

9/23/06: I can't believe that I haven't seen you at all in 2006. I know you must wonder where I am and what happened to our family. I may have written this before, but here it is again: In September of 2003, Lucinda told me that she had cancer again and needed radiation treatment. She said she would be radioactive and consequently couldn't be around you while she had treatments. I believed her and asked my parents to come to Florida to watch you while I worked. Mimi and Papa came to Florida to watch you while Daddy worked. While they were there, they received numerous phone calls from guys asking if Lucinda was married. Lucinda told me that she was staying with someone from the Catholic Church, so I called the church, and she wasn't staying with anyone from the church. She eventually called to check on you, so I asked her where she was, and she said the church, so I told her that I knew she was lying. Come to find out she was in a hotel with a guy named Lonny, having an affair. When she finally came home, she kicked me out of the house for no reason, so I had to go to a hotel. A week later, I had the car accident ... and she didn't even have cancer. Your mother is nothing but a huge liar. When I married her, I thought that she had only been married once — to Arthur, Cassandra's father — but she lied. She was married before that. You guys were told that I was dead.

10/02/06: Her first husband was guy with the last name Puntelello. See the 10/2/05 diary entry. I can't believe that I can't be with you and help you with your schoolwork and reading. Remember your Dad is a teacher. I wish I could be a part of your lives, but your mother is so selfish, she won't keep me informed as to what is going on.

10/03/06: I drove by our old house in Turner today, and it brought back many memories—how we used to mow the lawn on Daddy's riding lawnmower, and how we used to snowmobile on "Copper" around Turner. I missed all the fun we had there.

10/05/06: I have some things to tell you regarding the days and weeks after my accident. After my accident I was in Saint Joseph's Hospital for a couple of weeks. You guys were staying with Melody and Aaron Taylor, and supposedly Lucinda was staying with me at the hospital. This was not true. Lucinda was staying in hotels and drinking at bars with her boyfriend, Lonny. She didn't even check in with you guys for two weeks. I have all the records that back this up. I was in the hospital, and Lucinda ordered the doctors to take me off of life support, hoping that I would die. I surprised everyone by living. I was in a coma, and once I awoke, a doctor was on his knees, crossing himself, thanking God for helping him save my life. Lucinda came in and yelled at the doctor, saying all kinds of hurtful things to the doctor like, "Look what you have done to his children, giving them a father like that—without a leg."

The doctor told Lucinda that at least the boys would get the chance to know their father and be with him. The doctor didn't know that Lucinda was having affairs and had no intention of being with me or keeping our family together.

10/17/06: This is Cassandra's birthday. I didn't know if you knew this or not, but Cassandra was supposed to be born in jail; Lucinda was in jail while pregnant, but her parents, Meme and Pepe, got her out of jail to have the baby under house arrest. It is almost Halloween, and I haven't been able to be with you to celebrate Halloween, Bowdoin and Camden. You probably can't even remember when we celebrated Halloween together. This makes me very sad.

10/30/06: I called to see what you dressed up for Halloween as, but no one answered the phone so I couldn't talk with either one of you about Halloween. I have so much to tell you, and I miss you very much, and I love you both so much.

10/31/06: I called again at 2:30 p.m. to talk with you about Halloween, but no one answered. I left a message, but no one returned my call.

11/8/06: I received a copy of your first quarter report card from first grade today, Camden, and you are doing so well in everything. Way to go, Camden. I am so proud of you. I haven't received your first quarter report card yet, Bowdoin, but hopefully it will arrive soon, or I will call your teacher again.

11/14/06: I finally received your report card today Bowdoin, and you are doing great. I am so proud of you Bowdoin—way to go. I talked with your school today to let them know that I want pictures of both of you.

11/23/06: Happy Thanksgiving, Bowdoin and Camden. I haven't been with you for Thanksgiving since 2004, when you guys had Thanksgiving with me when I lived with my department head. I tried to have you last year when your mother was in jail, but her boyfriend at the time, Kelly, who is now her husband, wouldn't answer the phone, and Cassandra wouldn't put him on the phone so I could have you or at least talk with you. This holiday should be at least better for you, since your mother isn't in jail this Thanksgiving. I am thinking of you both, and I love you and miss you guys so much. I am thankful that you are alive.

11/27/06: I called to talk with guys today at 1:40 p.m. to see how your Thanksgiving was, but no one answered the phone. I left a message for you, which you will probably never get to hear. I will never give up trying to be part of your lives, Camden and Bowdoin.

12/7/06: I walked to the pond today and fed sixteen ducks, and this made me think of you guys and how much you liked to feed the ducks. We used to feed the ducks together and chase them around. I hope you guys can remember that.

I mailed you Christmas presents today, Camden and Bowdoin. It will be a year tomorrow since the last time we saw each other. I took you guys fishing, and Bowdoin caught a huge bass, and I have the picture of you both with the fish, which is the last picture that I have of you guys. I have asked your mother on numerous occasions to send me recent pictures and school pictures of you both, but she just ignores these requests. I am constantly thinking of you both and missing you tremendously!

12/22/06: Bowdoin, I am thinking of you a lot lately; I am feeding the deer, and the deer are so tame that they come right up to you. You used to love seeing the deer. You got so excited when the deer came, and you got to see them. I really hope that you can remember that. I am also feeding the ducks, and there are lots of ducks — usually more than forty every day. Camden, you liked feeding the ducks. You did too, Bowdoin. I haven't been allowed to see you guys for over a year. I try to arrange to see you, but your mother refuses. Merry Christmas, and God bless you, Camden and Bowdoin! I think of you both every day, and I miss you and love you every day. I hope that you received the presents that I sent you for Christmas. The gifts included numerous DVDs and two watches.

12/24/06: Merry Christmas, Bowdoin and Camden. I miss you guys so much. I was supposed to be with you over Christmas, but your mother refuses to let me see you. Aunt Julie, Uncle Mike, and your cousin Nicole were here, and they had gifts for you both, as did Mimi and Papa. I too have presents for you. I just wish you were here to celebrate with me. I am so sad that I am now crying because I am not with you. I hope that you think of me and remember me with warm thoughts in your mind and your heart. I miss you decorating the tree and opening your presents with me. I told your mother that I wanted to have you over Christmas break; she ignored me and refused.

1/4/07: I called and was allowed to speak with you both for a few minutes. I asked you about Christmas and wished you both a happy New Year. You guys didn't thank me for your Christmas presents from me; I hope that you liked them. I told you both that I loved and missed you both very much. I also told you that I talked with your teachers, Ms. Weber and Ms. Kramer, and you are both doing so well.

1/6/07: When I talked with you a couple of days ago, I heard you in the background, Camden, saying it was James on the phone. This hurt, Camden, because I am your Dad. You probably call Kelly McCane "Daddy" and "Dad" now. This hurts me so much, because your actions influence Bowdoin.

1/25/07: I received your report cards today, and you are both doing extremely well. I am so proud of you both. Camden, your teacher said that you need to work on writing clearer and not so messy. Take your time and write better. Do you practice? If you were with me, I would practice with you every day. Remember, your Dad is a teacher. Bowdoin, Ms. Weber said you are doing great. I am happy to see that you are both doing so well in school. I miss you and love you both very much.

2/10/07: Daddy has to once again have surgery; this will make twenty-two surgeries since my accident. This time, I have to have my bladder operated on because I have bladder stones. I also have kidney stones. The doctor said the reason that I have stones is because I was placed in a nursing home after my surgery and that I didn't get my leg after my accident. The doctor blames your mother for this. This inactivity caused stones to be created. I am thinking of you both so much. I hope that the surgery will go okay. I miss you both and love you so much!

2/14/07: I had surgery today through my penis to remove one bladder stone. The doctor had to use a laser to blast the stone. I will have a catheter for three days.

2/17/07: I bled some with the catheter in, and it hurt like hell removing it today. Papa and Mimi have helped me so much. We all miss you and love both so much. I know that your mother never lets you know when I call you or send you things. From now on, I will buy you both two cards for your birthdays, so you can at least one day see them and know that your Dad thinks of you all the time. Your Dad will start a new job teaching high school English at Gorham High School on Monday, February 26. Wish me luck.

2/18/07: I forgot to tell you in my last entry that I will have to have another surgery in June to remove more bladder stones, because the doctor couldn't get them all through the penis, so he will have to cut me open in June to remove the other four stones. That will make twenty-three surgeries.

3/2/07: I received a progress report from your teacher today, Bowdoin, and it says that you are performing above grade level and are doing well beginning to learn how to read. I received this from your kindergarten teacher, Ms. Weber. Bowdoin, I am so proud of you and am so happy to hear this news. I look forward to hearing about you, Camden, soon. I think of you both and miss you both every day. It is really snowing out today, and if you were here, we could play in the snow—make a snowman, have snowball fights, build snow forts, and go snowmobiling. I smile just thinking about this. You probably don't remember that we used to play in the snow when we all lived together in Turner, Maine. Camden and Bowdoin, Daddy loves you very much.

3/31/07: I have been thinking of you guys so much lately. Do you know what tomorrow is? It is opening day for fishing season, and this makes me think so much of both of you. I used to take you both fishing, and I taught you both how to fish. We used to have so much fun together when we went fishing, and we always caught fish. I used to take you fishing in Florida and in Maine. I wish that your mother would let me see you and go fishing with you. We used to have so much fun. I hope that you get to go fishing, and I hope that you both remember me and think of me. Remember that your Dad always loves you and misses you, Camden and Bowdoin!

4/08/07: I have been thinking of you both so much lately. I hope you had a great Easter. I remember so much hiding your eggs and Easter candy and helping you find them. It was so much fun for all of us. I miss that so much. I hope that you went to church. I received your third quarter report cards, and I am so proud of you, Camden and Bowdoin. You are both doing so well in school. I call you both once a week, but your mother refuses to let me talk with you or just refuses to answer the phone. This makes me so mad. Remember that your Dad will never give up, and I love you so much. I haven't seen you guys in over a year. I have tried to arrange time to see you, but your mother refuses. I don't know why she is so mean.

4/20/07: DHHS contacted me today about child support. I don't mind at all paying child support, but I would like to the ability to talk with you and see you! I don't know why your mother won't let me talk with you or see you. This is so frustrating.

4/29/07: I am thinking of you, Camden and Bowdoin, constantly. I am in therapy now, and I am beginning to walk so much better. I can't wait to show you. I am a long-term substitute teacher at Gorham High School, and your picture is on my desk. The students say that you both look a lot like me. I am so proud of you both. I miss and love you guys so much.

5/17/07: I just found out today that your mother was charged once again with a speeding violation and has to attend—once again—a traffic school. She was charged $85 again for her second speeding violation. I hope that she doesn't drive crazy with both of you in the car. I am worried about you both, and I am constantly thinking of you both and missing you, Camden and Bowdoin.

5/30/07: I called you today to wish you a happy birthday, Bowdoin, and to see if you got my card and present. I hope you did, and I hope that you liked it. I bet that your mother didn't even tell you that I called, and I also bet that she didn't even give you my card or present. I also bet that she lied and told you that your father even didn't call to talk with you on your birthday. All lies, Bowdoin. I hope that you had a great birthday and remember that I am constantly thinking of you and your brother. I love you both and miss you so much. I went fishing last weekend and caught a salmon, and I was thinking of both you so much, wishing that you were with me.

6/16/07: I just had my twenty-third surgery, Camden and Bowdoin, and I have been thinking of you so much, hoping that I would survive and be able to talk with you. I still remember after the car accident when you guys were brought to see me in the nursing home by your babysitters, and you said, Camden, "I told you, Bowdoin, that Daddy isn't dead." That meant so much to me, Camden. I survived this latest surgery. This one was on my bladder, in which I had large bladder stones removed. I was in the hospital for a week, and I tried to call you to let you know, but your mother never answered the phone, so I left a message for you explaining this and saying that I wanted and needed to speak with you. Your mother never returned my call.

6/30/07: Mimi called you today to say hello and to talk with you, but your mother refused to let you guys talk with your grandmother. I don't know why she is so hurtful. Mimi and Papa think of you guys a lot and miss and love you. I wish that you guys were allowed to talk with Mimi and Papa. I miss you and love you, Camden and Bowdoin. I have quite a few animals that you both would enjoy feeding and seeing: deer, chipmunks (which I have named), ducks, and fish.

8/9/07: I really hope that you both had a great Fourth of July! I miss you both so much. I have called a few times to talk with you, Camden and Bowdoin, but your mother refuses to answer the phone, or if she does, she tells me that you guys aren't there! This makes me so mad! I have found out that she is sometimes using her old name (Lucinda Philbrook) because companies are trying to find her because she owes them money. Capital One is now after her. I have been trying to get in touch with Deltona Elementary School to find out who your teachers are going to be for this year, but as of yet I haven't found out. I have really been thinking of you both, my sons.

Daddy knows a big day is coming next month…somebody's birthday. Now whose birthday is it? I know Camden James Richardson is going to be a snowman. "A snowman?" you say? A snowman, when you draw it, resembles the number eight, and you are going to be eight years old. I wish I could be with you and see you, but your mother refuses to let me a part of your life. I will never forget or give up on being with you, Camden and Bowdoin.

8/30/07: I called your cousin, Nicki, today to find out how her first day of school was. I tried to call you to find out about your first day of school, Camden and Bowdoin, but your mother refused to answer her cell phone. She would not return my call. I am so frustrated! I called your school and found out your teacher's names. Bowdoin's teacher, Mrs. Krotje, and Camden's teacher, Ms. Karczewski, have both e-mailed me, so I will keep abreast of your progress. I so wanted to hear your voices to discover what you guys thought about first and second grade and your teachers. Maybe someday your mother will let me be a part of your lives.

9/10/07: I sent your birthday card and present today, Camden. I really hope that you get it. I also sent you a note and a present, Bowdoin. I will again try to call you both and talk with you, if your mother ever answers her cell phone and actually lets me talk with you. Time will tell. This hurts me so much, my sons.

9/14/07: Camden and Bowdoin, I don't know when you will ever read this, but you guys used to love seeing all the animals at Mimi's and Papa's house—the deer and the ducks. Bowdoin, you used to really love the deer. I hope you guys can remember. Well now there are flocks of turkeys; there were just over thirty turkeys eating right next to me. You guys would get such a kick out of seeing this and feeding the turkeys. I went fishing last week and caught some brook trout and salmon. I used to take you guys fishing all the time. I hope that you remember that.

9/17/07: Happy birthday, Camden James! I called you today, but your mother refused to answer her cell phone, and since she won't give me the house phone number, I can't call there. I tried and tried to talk with you. This hurts me so much, Camden. I am crying writing this. I want you to know that you are constantly in my thoughts and prayers. Happy eighth birthday, Camden. Love, Daddy.

10/14/07: I have called you guys a few times to talk with you and to find out how you are and to learn about what is going on in your lives, but Lucinda refuses to answer the phone. How is school going? Are you playing any sports? I miss you and love you so much.

10/31/07: Happy Halloween, Bowdoin and Camden! What are you dressing up as? Remember when I used to dress up with you and go trick-or-treating? You probably can't, but I wish that you could remember. I love and miss you both very much.

11/17/07: I finally received your report cards from Deltona Elementary School today, and I am so proud of both my sons. Way to go, Camden and Bowdoin; you have made your Dad so proud! I just wish that you knew that I would help you any way that I can. Remember that I am a teacher as well as your father. I also received your first grade pictures, Bowdoin, and your second grade pictures, Camden. Boy, do I have two very handsome sons. I just wish that your mother had sent me your kindergarten picture, Bowdoin, and your kindergarten and first grade pictures, Camden. I guess it isn't enough for her to keep us apart, but she doesn't want me to know anything about you. I hope you have a great Thanksgiving. Remember a couple of years ago when you were both with me for Thanksgiving because your mother was in jail? We had so much fun. I smile every time that I think of it. I hope that you both are healthy and happy, and remember that your Dad thinks of you daily and misses and loves you both so much.

11/18/07: Yesterday was Papa's birthday. It wouldn't have killed your mother to have you guys call him to wish him a happy birthday. He and Mimi love you and miss you both so much. Remember the deer and the four-wheelers and snowmobiles you used to ride at their house? Tomorrow is my birthday, and I haven't talked with you guys on my birthday in five years. Why won't your mother have you guys call me? I don't expect you guys to know that my birthday is November 19; I don't blame you, Bowdoin and Camden. Lucinda or Cassandra certainly could have told you and called me for you.

11/20/07: Yesterday was my birthday, and I spent the entire day thinking of you, Camden and Bowdoin! I just wish that I could have talked with you. That would have been the best present.

11/23/07: Yesterday was Thanksgiving, and I thought about you both all day, and everyone who was here also thought about you. Mimi said grace and thanked God that you two were alive and wished that you two could be a part of our lives. It brought tears to my eyes. I called you both today, but your mother refuses to answer her cell phone when I call. She refuses to give me your home phone number, which is illegal, because it goes against the judge's order and the divorce decree. I can and will show you this whenever I get to see you. I give thanks everyday that you two are my sons. Love and prayers, your father—Daddy.

11/26/07: I am thinking about you a lot this time of year, with it being the holiday season. I wish I could be with you to experience the holidays together. Watching the Christmas specials on TV and singing Christmas carols and going to church to pray to our savior

Jesus Christ—that is what Christmas is all about. I can't believe Lucinda won't let us at least talk with each other. I love you and miss you, Bowdoin and Camden, and you are both in my prayers every day.

12/1/07: Camden and Bowdoin, I can't believe that your mother has stolen everything from me! I am not even talking about material things; that list is too long to write down, but if you are interested some day, I think that you will be shocked to learn about everything. What I am talking about is my relationship with you both. I hope you can remember all the things that we used to do together and all that I used to do with and for you. I used to coach you both in baseball and basketball, and I taught you both how to ride your first bikes. I used to be the one who bathed you both, and we used to go fishing at least twice a week all year round. We also used to go shopping, because your mother hated to go shopping with you, but we always had so much fun shopping. We made a game out of it. I hope you can remember.

It is the season for Christmas shopping, and I am sad because we can't go shopping together to play our shopping games. It has almost been two years since we last saw each other, and this time a year was so special for us because we always did all the decorating around the house, making it feel like the holiday season. We used to make paper Christmas decorations (chains, sockets, snowmen and Santas), and we used to sing Christmas carols. I hope that you can remember this.

I try to call you both all the time, but Lucinda refuses to answer her cell phone, and I bet she doesn't even allow you guys to listen to my messages. I also bet that she lies about me constantly and bad-mouths me in front of you guys. All lies, Camden and Bowdoin. I love you and miss you both terribly. I just wish that we could see each other, or at least talk with each other. I don't know why she is so hateful and mean. I never did anything bad to her. She is the one who broke up our family!

12/15/07: I went Christmas shopping for you guys today, and I got you some things that I sent out today. I hope that your mother will let you have them. I hope she doesn't send the gifts back like she did before. I sent you both brief notes and notices of your savings bonds that I got you. I just wish that you both could read. I know it's close; you will be both reading soon, so maybe you can get the mail and read it before your mother sees it and throws it away without letting you know that your father writes to you and calls you often. I don't understand why she is so mean. She is only hurting you, my sons.

It has been two years since we last saw each other. I try all the time to arrange times when we could see each other, but your mother either ignores me or refuses. Camden and Bowdoin, please know that your Dad will never give up trying to be a part of your lives. It does hurt me so much that she doesn't follow the law and let me be a part of your lives. I have taken her back to court two times, and all the court has done is slap her on the wrist, and it has cost well over $5,000 both times; I just don't have that kind of money to waste. I know that she lies to you both about me and bad-mouths me in front of you. I know she has worked hard to turn you against your own father. I know this because she did the same thing to Cassandra about her father, Arthur. God bless you, Bowdoin and Camden, and please remember that your Dad misses and loves you terribly.

12/23/07: I called using a calling card today to speak with you, but your mother refused to let me speak with you guys unless I gave her a phone number, which she already has, because it showed up on her caller ID. She called back and refused to let me speak with you. Mimi got on the phone and said hi to both of you. This hurts Mimi and Papa so much. It is killing them, seeing how badly this is hurting me. I can't let her kill your grandparents — my parents. They have been there for me every day since the accident and since I lost my leg, and I won't let Lucinda hurt my parents, who are really getting old. She complained about how I haven't been paying child support for you — how quickly she forgets the $50,000 she stole from me. I really pray that you have a great Christmas, and remember that your Dad loves you and is there for you. I wish I could know what sports and clubs you are involved in, but your mother refuses to let me know. She refuses to send me pictures of my sons. How mean can anyone be?

12/29/07: I really hope that you both had a great Christmas, and remember that your Dad is thinking about you and missing you constantly. I have some news to tell you. I bought you a new kitten, which I was to have you guys name, but your mother refuses to let me speak with you, so I named it Sebec. She is a great kitten—twelve weeks old and very playful. I hope that you both can see it and play with it soon. I sent your mother a letter with my address and phone number on it, as she demanded, even though she already knew my address and phone number. Supposedly, she will now set up a schedule so we can talk with each other every week. She has said this before, so I am not holding my breath. Hopefully she with live up to this promise.

1/1/08: Happy New Year, Camden and Bowdoin! I really hope that this year will bring us closer together.

1/15/08: I called today to talk with you, but Lucinda refused unless I sent her a letter with my address and phone number on it. She already has my address and phone number. I argued with her, but she would not allow me to speak with you, so I sent her a letter with my address and phone number on it. She promised that if I did that, she would set up a schedule so I could talk with you every week. I am still waiting for that schedule and to talk with you.

1/21/08: I called to talk with you, Bowdoin and Camden, but your mother refuses to answer the phone when I call. I knew that you didn't have school today, since it is Martin Luther King Day, so I wanted to talk with you both and to let you know, Bowdoin, that I talked with your teacher and principal a couple of days ago. Everything is going to well with speech therapy that your teacher believes that you will no longer need an IEP, or Individualized Education Program. I am so proud of you, Bowdoin.

Camden, you are doing great in school, and I wish that I could talk with to tell you that I am proud of you and to let you know everything that Mrs. Karczewski told me about you on the phone.

This makes me so sad that I can't even talk with my sons, let alone see you. I don't know why your mother is so hateful toward me. I never did anything wrong or bad toward her. Unlike Lucinda , I never stole thousands of dollars, or all her personal possessions from her, like she did from me. I never cheated on her with other people like she did to me. You will understand this when you get older.

1/27/08: I wanted to talk with you today and tell you that I am nervous; I start a new job tomorrow as a long-term history and social studies teacher. It is okay if you guys get nervous, especially when you are about to do something unfamiliar and new to you. I guess I wanted you to know that I am constantly thinking of you, and that I want to be part of your lives. I am here for you, and I am sad and mad that your mother refuses to let me be part of your lives. I hope and know deep in my heart that you guys want to be a part of my life, too. I know that Lucinda tells you nothing but lies about me, like, "Your father never calls," and, "Your father, or James, doesn't do anything for you." All lies, Camden and Bowdoin.

2/3/08: Today is the Super Bowl, and I am thinking of you both so much today and wishing that I could see the game with you so we could cheer on our New England Patriots together. I wish that I could call you and talk with you, but your mother refuses to let your Dad be a part of your lives. Why is she so mean?

2/10/08: Bowdoin I received your report card, and I am so proud of you! You are certainly mastering first grade. I called to congratulate you and tell you about the present that I bought you, but your mother refused to answer the phone, so I left a message, which you will never get. Camden, I haven't received your report card yet, so I e-mailed your teacher. I think it should be coming soon. I am sure that you are doing well, but I can't wait see it. I love you both and miss you both so much.

2/16/08: I am really mad today, Camden and Bowdoin! I tried to call you and talk with you, but your mother has had the number disconnected. I also tried Cassandra's cell phone, and that number has been disconnected as well. I don't have a land line number for you because Lucinda refuses to give it to me.

2/20/08: Camden, I finally received your report card today. I am so proud of you—honor roll. All As and one B. You only went down in reading. I know you can bring it back up. I just wish that I could talk with you and Bowdoin to tell you how proud I am of you. You two mean the world to me. I just pray that your mother will develop a conscience and a heart and do the right thing and let me be a part of your lives. I don't even care that she stole everything from me—all my personal possessions and my leg. What I care about is that she stole you from me.

2/26/08: Camden and Bowdoin, I went to court today, and I agreed to pay child support of $370 per month. I prepaid child support of over $30,000 at the time of the divorce, and I am sure that you never received a penny of that money, for your mother spent it on a vehicle, her breasts (augmentation), and having many of her scars removed. I also bet that she told you that I don't pay child support, which is a blatant lie. In fact, my lawyer argued that I could fight paying child support, for I had previously paid such an exorbitant amount, but I disagreed with my lawyer. I want you both to have everything that I can possibly give you. The sad part is that I can't ensure that you will ever see anything from this money, because it goes to Lucinda, and I can't make her spend it on you.

3/4/08: Bowdoin, I received your first semester report card today and you are doing great. I am so proud of you and your brother. Your Daddy loves you and Camden so much. I wish that your mother would let me talk with you and see you both.

4/10/08: I paid my second child support payment today of $370. I paid $370 last month, but I bet that you didn't see a dime of that money; moreover, I bet that you won't see anything from this money, either. It is too bad that your mother won't let me talk to or see you both. I am constantly thinking about you both, Camden and Bowdoin. I love you and miss you both so much that hurts!

4/21/08: I received your third-quarter report card today, Bowdoin and you are doing so great. You improved in everything. I still haven't received your report card, Camden; I can't wait to get it. I wish that I could talk with both you of you to let you know that your Dad is constantly thinking about you and missing you both so much, but your mother refuses to let me talk to you. I love you and miss you, Camden and Bowdoin.

4/26/08: I went fishing today at Thompson Lake with Glenn and Paul, and I caught two salmon. One was twenty-two inches long, and the other was eighteen inches. I caught them on a streamer fly. I was only the only one who caught fish, and I was the only one fishing flies. The other two guys were fishing live bait—smelts. I was thinking of you both the entire time, remembering how we used to go fishing all the time and wishing that I could be with you to teach you how to fly fish. You would have had a great time, and I wish that you two were with me.

5/06/08: Camden, I finally received your third quarter report card today, and I also received your progress report and Bowdoin's progress report for the fourth quarter. You are both doing well, but you both need to work on your handwriting neatness. I just wish that I could be with you to help you both work on this. I am sure that your mother doesn't work with you on this. Remember that your Dad is a teacher and knows how to help you work on these things, but your mother refuses to let me talk with you or help you on this. She does this because she wants to hurt me, but she is only hurting you both. Your grades are good, Camden, and your Dad is so proud of you both. I miss you and love you, Camden and Bowdoin.

5/11/08: Bowdoin and Camden, Daddy went fishing today at Moose Pond, and I caught six salmon. Two were huge—twenty-five and twenty-four inches. The other four were nice, too. I thought of you both all day today, wishing that you were with me. You guys would have had so much fun catching fish with your dad. I can't believe that your mother won't let you see me and be with me. I pay $370 a month in child support, but I bet that you guys don't see a penny of that money. I also bet that she tells you that I don't give any money for you. All lies. You will discover this soon. You are both constantly in my thoughts and my prayers. Love, Daddy.

5/15/08: I paid my third child support payment today—$370,

with instructions for your mother to get you anything that you want for your birthday, Bowdoin, and to tell you that this is from Daddy. I bet that she didn't get you a thing from me, and I bet that you and Camden never see a dime of that money that I send to you every month. This irritates the hell out of me!

5/28/08: Daddy bought a boat a couple of days ago—a fourteen-foot, 1971 Starcraft Falcon with a 1988 twenty-horse Evenrude. I named the boat after you and my cat: Sebec/Bowdoin/Camden. I hope that I can see you soon and take you both out on it so we can go fishing and swimming. I am thinking of you both constantly. Love, Daddy.

5/30/08: Happy birthday, Bowdoin! Happy seventh birthday! I called you today at 3:30 to wish you a happy birthday and to talk with you, but Lucinda refused to answer the phone when I called. I am sure that she told you and continues to tell you that I didn't call and that I don't care about you and Camden. These are nothing but utter lies. This hurts me so much, Bowdoin and Camden. I sincerely hope that you had a great day, and in your heart of hearts, that you know that your Dad is constantly thinking of you, missing you, and loving you.

6/15/08: I was hoping that you would call today to wish me a happy father's day and to talk with your Dad, but you didn't. I don't blame you; your mother should have had you call me today, but she didn't. I shouldn't be surprised. I received your final report card yesterday, and I wanted to congratulate you and talk with you about it. You both did so well in first and second grades. Your father is so proud of you, Camden and Bowdoin. Daddy bought a boat, and I wanted to talk with you about it and about going fishing. It is a nice boat, and we can go fishing and swimming from it safely. I love you and miss you both so much.

7/12/08: Bowdoin and Camden, Daddy has so much to tell you. I got your last report card for your first and second grades, and you guys did so well. I am very proud of you both. I sold my motorcycle a couple of days ago. This made me sad because I wanted you both to see it and go for a ride on it with me. I sent you a picture of it, and I hope that you got to see it. I wish you could go out on my boat with me, fishing. Please remember that I am constantly thinking of you both and wishing that I could be a part of your lives, but your mother refuses. I pay so much money in child support, and she still won't let me see you or talk with you, which is against the law.

7/30/08: I can't believe that you came to see me today, Bowdoin and Camden! I wish that I had known you were here in Maine—I can't believe that you had been here in Maine for two weeks. If I had known, I would have taking you fishing with me. We could have done so many things—fun things. We could have gone fishing on my boat.

7/31/08: I wish that your mother had told me that you were both in Maine and have been here for two weeks so I could have spent some time with you. We could have spent some quality time together. You are leaving Maine in a couple of hours. I haven't seen you since December 8, 2005! Why couldn't your mother have called me to let me know that you were both in Maine? I miss you and love you both so much.

8/2/08: I am so irate at your mother for not telling me that you were in Maine and for not telling me anything about both of you. I didn't know that you broke your arm last year, Camden, or that you have been playing football. I would like to talk to you about it and come see a few games. Bowdoin, did you know that your Daddy took karate lessons, too? I would have liked to have known so I could talk with you about it. Why is your mother so mean and hurtful toward me? I have never done anything to hurt her. She can't obviously say the same thing in regards to me.

8/16/08: Camden and Bowdoin, I wish that you two would occasionally call me to talk with me, for I miss you both so much! I call Lucinda's cell phone, but she screens the call and refuses to answer the phone, so I leave messages that I bet you never get to hear. Why don't you return my calls? I think I know it is because your mother never tells you that your Dad calls. Why is she such a female dog?

9/1/08: Camden and Bowdoin, Daddy went fishing in Rangeley this weekend, and I caught brook trout and salmon. Do you remember that I took you to Rangeley before we moved to Florida? Do you remember the fish that we all caught in those ponds? I have pictures of us fishing there.

I learned who your teachers are this year. Bowdoin, you have Camden's teacher from last year, Ms. Karczewski, and Camden, you have Mrs. Pinkava. I have e-mailed both of them, and I will be in contact with both of them to find out what is going on, because your mother refuses to let me know anything about your school happenings or anything about you. I love and miss you both so much.

9/17/08: Camden, I have thinking about you all day! It's your birthday. I went fishing today, and I thought of you because we always used to go fishing together, and we had so much fun. I hope you can remember. I caught five bass today. I wanted to catch nine to match your birthday. I called you today, and your mother answered the phone, and I wished you a happy birthday. You were at the Boston Red Sox game at Tropicana Field. Do you remember the time that I brought you to Fenway Park to see the Red Sox? Probably not—you were so young. You could barely hear me on the phone because of all the noise at the game. Too bad the Red Sox lost, but maybe you are a Rays fan now. I asked to speak with Bowdoin, but your mother refused.

10/3/08: I want you, Camden and Bowdoin, to know that my wages at Hannaford have been garnished $87.50 per week for child support, which equates to $370.00 a month. I bet that you guys don't see a dime of that money, and I also bet that she tells you that I don't pay anything for child support. All lies! I wish she would have you guys call me.

10/31/08: Happy Halloween, Bowdoin and Camden. I wish I could see you and be with you for Halloween. I would dress up in a costume and go trick-or-treating with you. We used to go trick-or-treating together, Camden. I never had the chance to go with you, Bowdoin, because you were too young, and then my accident happened, and your mother wouldn't let me have you guys for the Halloween holiday. I hope you realize that I am thinking of you both and missing you both. Your dad loves you so much.

11/02/08: Camden I got your third grade, first quarter report card today, and I am very proud of you—all As and one B for reading.

I wish I was with you to work on your reading with you. We could read all kinds of books together.

11/10/08: Camden and Bowdoin, I received your pictures today, and your grades for the first quarter, Bowdoin. I was shocked to see that you had a cast on your arm, Camden. Daddy had no idea that you were hurt and had a broken right arm. I called your mother, but she refused to let me speak with you, Camden.

11/20/08: I am so sad today, Bowdoin and Camden. Yesterday was my birthday, and I was hoping to receive a birthday card or a telephone call from you, but I didn't receive anything. This makes six straight years that I haven't talked with you guys or even received a card from you. I don't blame you, but I do blame your mother. She could have at least had you call your dad on his birthday, but she didn't. Why is she so mean?

11/27/08: Happy Thanksgiving, Camden and Bowdoin. I really miss you guys so much. I am so thankful that you are my sons. I haven't been with you on Thanksgiving since 2004, when we were together at my friend Jill's house. I tried to have you in 2005, when your mother was in jail, but Kelly McCane refused to let me have you. I am so proud of you both. You're both doing well in school. I wish I could have some pictures of you playing sports—football and karate. I don't know why your mother won't send me any pictures of you. Why? Why? Why? I wish I could at least have your e-mail addresses so I could at least communicate with you.

12/6/08: I sent you guys a Christmas card today and a present; I got you both savings bonds, and I asked you to send me your e-mail addresses so I could write you and send you pictures. I bet you won't even see it. I love you and miss you both so much.

12//20/08: I called you both today, Camden and Bowdoin to wish you a Merry Christmas and to see whether or not you received my Christmas card and presents, but your mother refused to answer the phone, so I left you a message. Your mother didn't have you guys call me back. I miss you and love you both so much. It makes me so sad that I can't see you and talk with you. I give your mother $87.50

a week for child support, but she refuses to let me be a part of your lives.

12/23/08: I called again today to talk with you, and I was allowed to speak with you both, and this made me so happy. I told you both that I am very proud of you and your accomplishments in school. Camden, you told me that you played fullback, and that football season just ended, and you are going to play baseball when baseball season starts. It was nice to talk with you, too, Bowdoin, and you were happy to talk with your Dad.

12/27/08: I am thinking about you both so much this time of year. I can't believe another Christmas has come and gone, and I am not allowed to be with you. It has now been three years since I have been with you for a Christmas celebration. I am sure you can't even remember decorating my tree and receiving your gifts with me in 2005. This makes me so sad. I hope you have a great New Year, and I sincerely wish that 2009 will bring changes in your mother so we can spend more time together.

1/2/09: Happy New Year, Camden and Bowdoin. I hope I get to see you, talk with you, and be with you this year.

1/14/09: Guess who I spent time with today? Sydney and Avery Taylor. I hope you remember who they are. You both used to spend tons of time together with them both in Maine and Florida. I have written about them before in this diary. See entries dated 7/1/06 and 7/20/06 to refresh your memory. They are doing great. It made me feel great to be with them. I helped Sydney do her math homework, and this made me really think of both of you. I wish I could be with you to help you with your homework and be a part of your lives. Knowing that your mother refuses to let me be a part of your lives hurts me so much. Avery and Sydney still call me Uncle James, and this makes me feel good. If I could see you here in Maine, I would take you so you could visit with them.

1/16/09: Camden and Bowdoin, Daddy is very sad today. I have been thinking a lot about you both and how much I have missed and continue to miss in your lives. I don't even know your friends; who are they, and what are they like? What do you like to do with them? I get reports from your school so I know that you are doing well academically, but I have no idea about your athletic endeavors; moreover, I could have helped you practice for your sporting events. This makes me so sad, because before my accident, I used to coach you both in baseball and basketball. I hope that you can remember that. I could have helped you with your homework, and in the future, I could have helped you with girls. I will end up missing everything. I wish that your mother would let you call me and ask anything that you want or call me just to talk, but she won't, and she never answers the phone when I call or lets you guys return my calls.

1/28/09: Camden, I got your second quarter report card today. I still haven't received your report card, Bowdoin. Camden, Daddy is so proud of you—all As and Bs! I just wish that I could be with you to tell you and show you how proud I am of you. You went down one point in spelling and four points in science, but you went up one point in reading, two points in math, and one point in writing. I like to write, and I am in the process of writing a book that I will definitely let you read. I love you and miss you both so very much.

2/12/09: Hey guys. I am thinking of you both a lot lately. Bowdoin, you really got shortchanged in getting to know me, for my accident happened when you were only two years old. At least Camden can remember his real Dad, but I am not convinced that you can even remember me, Bowdoin. This makes me so sad. I hope and pray every day that you both know that your Dad loves you and misses you both, and not a day goes by that I don't think of you.

2/23/09: Hi boys. I am really worried about you. I just learned that your mother filed charges against Kelly for domestic violence that you both witnessed. He hits her. I hope you realize that this is wrong; it is never right to hit a girl. I hope that he isn't hitting you.

2/25/09: Camden and Bowdoin, I found out yesterday that 's Lucinda husband, Kelly McCane, has been charged with domestic violence. I am so worried about you both. I contacted both of your teachers today—Ms. Karczewski and Ms. Pinkava—to let them know what is going on. Since no one informs me about what is going on, I let your school know what is happening so they can keep an eye on you both to ensure that you are both all right.

3/5/09: Bowdoin and Camden, I learned today that one of your half-sisters, Cassandra Philbrook, is following in her mother's foot-steps. She now has a criminal record for shoplifting. This occurred yesterday at Wal-Mart. She also has traffic violations for not having her vehicle registered. I hope all is well with you both, and Daddy is constantly thinking of you, missing you, and loving you both.

4/7/09: Bowdoin and Camden, Daddy called you today on your spring vacation from school to talk with you and to see how you are, but your mother refused to answer the phone, so I left you a message that I bet you never got to hear. I wanted to ask you if you are okay and to make sure that Kelly McCane isn't hurting you. I know that he had to go to court for domestic violence charges, for he hit your mom. I hope he hasn't been hitting you. I know that Cassandra had to go to court for stealing from Wal-Mart. The apple doesn't fall far from the tree. I am sure that she learned that behavior from her mother. I am getting ready for fishing season, and I wish that you were both with me so I could take you fishing on my boat so we could catch salmon and trout together.

4/12/09: Happy Easter, Camden and Bowdoin. Daddy is think-ing of you both today, and I wish that you were with me so we could celebrate Easter together.

4/13/09: I called today you both today at 5:40 p.m. to talk with you about fishing, but your mother refused to answer the phone, so I left you a message telling you that I loved and missed you both so much and I wished that you were with me so I could take you fish-ing tomorrow.

4/28/09: I got your third quarter report cards today, and you both did well, but your grades went down, Bowdoin. I can't help but think that it is because of all the things that you witnessed this quar-ter—the domestic violence, and all the legal problems that Cassan-dra has gone through—have created so much tension in your living conditions. This really worries me, Bowdoin and Camden. I wish that you were both with me so you could focus on school and what is important to you rather than what you have had to deal with in terms of Kelly and Cassandra.

5/18/09: Camden and Bowdoin, I pay $370 per month in child support to the state of Florida, and they give that money to your mother, and she is supposed to use it on you. Your Daddy does this so you can get whatever it is that you might need: clothes, health care, and even toys. I bet that your mother tells you that your Dad doesn't pay child support. This nothing but a bald-faced lie! She used to do the same thing to Cassandra about her father, Arthur Philbrook.

That is not all, Camden and Bowdoin. I have arranged for you to get monthly Social Security checks for $742, which once again, your mother is supposed to spend on you. I am willing to bet that neither of you sees a penny of all this money that your Dad is getting you. If you were with me and living with me, I would set up bank accounts in your names, and you could get the money anytime that you wanted it.

5/23/09: Camden and Bowdoin, I called the Hernando County Sheriff's Department today, and I spoke with Deputy Lamia. I told him that I had no idea where you guys were, for I saw on the computer that Lucinda had been evicted from where she was living, but I had no idea that she wasn't living at the 9683 Baldridge Road address with Kelly McCane. I told Deputy Lamia this, and I gave her cell phone number, and I left a message for Lucinda to call me. The deputy found her and made her call me, and she finally gave me her new address, which she said was 4900 Canonball Court, Spring Hill, Florida, 34609. She also said that she had been living there since the domestic violence case that she had tried against Kelly McCane. I researched this address, and the house is for sale; it is under foreclosure.

5/30/09: Happy Birthday, Bowdoin! I called you today, and I was allowed to speak with you and wish you a happy birthday. You said that you loved me and missed me, and I told you the same thing. Lucinda wouldn't let me speak to you, Camden, but your dad loves and misses you too.

6/22/09: Yesterday was Father's Day, and I hoped and wished that you guys would have called me to wish me a happy Father's Day so I could have talked with my sons. I don't blame you, but I do blame your mother for not having you guys call me. You're both too young to locate the number and call long distance, but Lucinda could have helped you call me. It has now been six years since we spoke on Father's Day, and it makes me very sad.

7/4/09: Happy Fourth of July, Camden and Bowdoin! I wish we could be together to celebrate America's birthday. We would have so much fun going to parades and the fireworks and playing all sorts of games. I miss you and love you both so much.

8/18/09: Lucinda e-mailed me on 8/11/09, telling me that she now has another new cell phone number. I e-mailed her months ago, and she finally responded to my e-mail. I didn't even know her e-mail address, I just guessed what it was. She said that you were both at baseball camp last week, and that you would call me over the weekend. She lied about having you call me, because you never called. I would have loved to have talked to you about baseball camp. I used to coach you both in baseball at the Y before my accident. I just hope that you can remember that.

9/2/09: Lucinda called me today to inform me that she has once again moved with you. Your new address is now 9526 Northern Charm Square, Brooksville, Florida, 34613. I looked into it and discovered that she has once again been evicted from the Canonball address. By my count, you guys have moved four times since my accident. I am so sorry that your mother never pays her bills. Lord knows that I give her enough money—well over a thousand bucks a month. I got to talk to you both, and you are scared because now you will have to go to a new school. I wish that you were both with me, because I would never let anything like this happen. Don't be scared; your Dad is with you, and I won't let anything bad happen to you if I know about it.

9/16/09: Camden and Bowdoin your teachers at Deltona Elementary School e-mailed me today to inform me that you no longer attend that School. They said that you now go to Pine Grove

Elementary School. I called that school and discovered that your teacher is Ms. Maher, Camden and Bowdoin your teacher is Ms. Calderone. The telephone number of the school is 352–797–7090.

9/17/09: I called to wish you a happy birthday today Camden and no one answered the phone so I left a message and soon thereafter Lucinda returned my call so that I could talk with you. You seemed happy to get a basketball hoop and ball. I told you that I love you, and miss you and that I know that you are now going to a new school. I wish that your mother would one day follow the divorce decree and inform me about changes in your lives. I learned that you have been going to the new school since 9/8/09.

10/6/09: Camden your teacher, Mrs. Maher e-mailed me today to inform me that you were student of the week last week. She also e-mailed me pictures of you showing beside the sign that you were in fact student of the week. This made me so happy and proud of you. Bowdoin I also received a message from your teacher, Ms. Calderone so now I know your 4th and 3rd grade teachers at Pine Grove Elementary School.

10/7/09: I called to speak with you Camden and Bowdoin, but your mother refused to answer the phone so I left a message for you. I congratulated you Camden for winning/being student of the week last week at school. I told you both that I am thinking of you and that I love you both.

10/21/09: I called tonight at 7:05 p.m. to talk with you guys as previously arranged with Lucinda that we would be able to talk every Wednesday night. She said that she would have you guys call me, but Lucinda didn't do it last week so I called this week, but Lucinda refused to answer the phone so I left a message for you both Camden and Bowdoin, but I bet that you guys never get to hear any of the messages that I left for you.

10/29/09: I called tonight at 7:05 p.m. to talk with you Camden and Bowdoin and once again your mother refused to answer the phone so I left a message for you both. I love and miss you both dearly.

11/6/09: I received your first quarter report cards today and I am so proud of you both. Camden congratulations on being on the Honor Roll and I know that you will get next quarter Bowdoin. If you were with me I would work on your reading every day. I tried calling you both two times before Halloween to see what you were dressing up as, but your mother refused to answer the phone and she refused to have you guys call me back. It hurts me so much but I try not to think about it. Camden do you remember when your Daddy took you trick or treating and we both dressed up as devils? Bowdoin I never got the chance to take you trick or treating because you were too young (only 2) and then I had my accident.

11/07/09: I called today at 1:45 p.m. to congratulate you both on your report cards and to tell you how proud I am of you both, but your mother refused to answer the phone so I left a message for you both.

11/20/09: Thank you both so much for calling me yesterday on my birthday. You both definitely made my day. I am so glad that you are going fishing and catching fish. I wish that we could go fishing together on my boat. Camden I am so proud of you for being in writer's club and I will e-mail your teacher to tell her as well.

11/26/09: I called today at 11:15 a.m. to wish you a happy Thanksgiving Camden and Bowdoin and to tell you Camden that I received your second quarter progress report and to tell you and Bowdoin that Sydney and Avery Taylor say hi and that they both miss you.

11/29/09: I called today at 2:10 p.m. to talk with you and to see how your Thanksgiving was, but once again Lucinda refused to answer the phone, so I left a message which I'm sure that you will never get to hear. Your Dad misses you and loves you both so much and it hurts me that we never get to talk with each other.

12/3/09: I have been thinking so much about you both lately. I am having trouble sleeping because I feel that I am missing so much. I have been thinking about what I was doing as a child your age. When I was 8 and 10 years old my Dad would practice baseball with me every week. Hitting me hard ground balls to field and fly balls to catch and pitching me baseballs to hit were just some of the things he would do to make me a better baseball player. This would continue for years to come and I think that it is the main reason that I started as a freshman for my varsity high school baseball team. If you guys were with me I would practice your sports activities with you every day and I would help you study so that you could get so much more out of school. I just miss you both so much. Lucinda called the other day and said that you don't remember Sydney and Avery, but I know for fact that you do Camden and I bet that you remember them too Bowdoin. After all you were both told by Lucinda that I was dead when you were ages two and four and Camden I remember to this day when I saw you both in the nursing when your babysitters took you to see me and you said Camden "I told you Bowdoin that Daddy is not dead." I have to thank your babysitters Jasmine and Billy Fagen for not believing that I was dead.

12/24/09: Camden and Bowdoin I called tonight to wish you a Merry Christmas but your mother refused to answer the phone. I called at 6:15 p.m. and I left you a message telling you that I hoped and prayed that you would have a great Christmas. I miss you and love you both so much.

1/03/10: I can't believe I got to actually see you on December 30, 2009. It was only for 10 minutes but it meant so much to me. You two have certainly changed a lot since I last saw you. I can't believe that your mother didn't tell me that you were coming to Maine and that you had been here for a week before she actually called to tell me that you were in Maine. She refused to even let me know that she was bringing you to my house to see me. Thank God that I was there. When I talked to her on the phone I asked her if I could come get you so I could spend some time with you, but she adamantly refused; moreover she said that I couldn't see you alone without her. Once again she blatantly ignores the divorce decree, but I am so happy that I at least got to see you for 10 minutes.

1/08/10: I called today at 6:50 p.m. to talk with you and again she didn't answer the phone and I couldn't leave a message because her voice mail box was full.

1/10/10: I called again to talk with you and of course she didn't answer the phone so I left a message for you wishing you both a

Happy New Year and telling you that your Dad misses and loves you both very much.

1/23/10: I called at 8:00 p.m. to talk to you but your mother refused to answer the phone so I left a message telling you that I missed you and loved you both so much.

1/30/10: I called tonight at 7:00 p.m. to talk to you Camden and Bowdoin but your mother refused to answer the phone so I left a message telling your mother that I sent her a letter and that I e-mailed her attempting to set up a time that I could talk with you on weekly basis so that we could keep in contact with each other. I also left a message telling you that I loved you and missed you both so much.

2/4/10: Camden I got your fourth grade second quarter report card today and you did great. You went up in reading to an A from a B. You only went down in spelling to a C from an A. You will bring that up next time. Happy New Year Camden and Bowdoin! I have called you numerous times but your mother refuses to answer the phone.

2/13/10: I called you today at 5:45 p.m. to wish you a happy Valentine's Day, but your mother refused to answer the phone so I left a message for you and her. I said to her that she must have received my letter and my e-mails to her for us to set up a time when I could call you and talk with you and I told her to have you guys call me. I love you and miss you both so much. I got your report card Bowdoin and Daddy is so proud of you and Camden. Love, Dad.

2/17/10: I called today at 6:00 p.m. to talk to you Camden and Bowdoin, but your mother refused to answer the phone. I am getting so tired of this and I bet that you never get to hear the messages that I leave for you. This is so frustrating for me Camden and Bowdoin. Your Dad is trying so hard to be a part of your lives, but your mother refuses to let me be a part of it. I love you and miss you both so much.

Appendix B

James Richardson
481 West Elm Street
Yarmouth, ME 04096
207–846–3450
1/6/09
Department of Health and Human Services
116 State House Station
Augusta, ME 04333–01666
Attn: Carol Oxley

Dear Ms. Oxley:

As per our phone conversation today, here is that letter. I finally saw Mr. Margulis — whose first name I forget, perhaps Martin — on December 29, 2008, at his office (if it can be called that) in Freeport. It is a house — his private residence — rather than an office. I parked in the driveway, and thank God I brought my parents with me. My father went to the door to determine whether or not we were in the right place, and Mr. Margulis came to the door to tell him we were in the right place, and for me to walk out front to enter the house. I did, and the steps were huge concrete slabs with no rails. I guess that Martin is not familiar with the A.D.A. There was no way that I could enter this "office" without the help of my father.

Once I got into this office, Mr. Margulis was not at all concerned about me or my parents; he was concerned with lumber he was having delivered. He was totally unprofessional and never introduced himself or greeted my parents. Perhaps his lumber was more important than common courtesy, saying hello to my mother and father. There was no waiting room for us to sit in, and my parents were told that they could not stay and had to move my car from the premises because of the lumber coming.

Mr. Margulis told them to drive around for forty-five minutes, and then they could return. Gas prices have gone down, but not enough to waste like this. He refused to talk with me on the ground floor because people were moving things to get prepared for the arrival of lumber. My parents left, and he asked me to go upstairs to meet with him in his "office." There was a plethora of narrow stairs I had to maneuver to meet with him in his office, which was a bedroom.

I am physically disabled; I lost my left leg above the knee and have rods in my left arm, and my right wrist is fused. It seems to me that he must have been—or at least should have been—aware of my physical limitations. I believe I was forced to see him so he could determine my mental limitations. No rails, no elevator, and he was to meet with the public in his private residence? There seems to be a problem here. Once I got upstairs, he began his "session" by saying, "You seem to have anger issues."

I have fallen and broken my collarbone in the past, and irregular ground scares me. I was angry that he had no rails and didn't seem to care what I had to go through to enter his "office." He was disrespectful to my parents, telling them that they had to leave.

Why couldn't they stay in the waiting room? Oh yeah — there was no waiting room. It seems to me that the state or federal government must have someone else to whom they could send people to determine whether or not they are eligible for supplemental security income.

Mr. Margulis said, "You don't seem disabled. Why are you attempting to get SSI disability?"

I told him that I was a teacher with over fourteen years of teaching experience. I am disabled, and I no longer had a teaching job and am unable to secure a teaching position because of my physical and mental disabilities. I should have countered his question with a question of my own: "Are you familiar with the Americans with Disabilities Act, or do you just willfully ignore it?"

Ms. Oxley, I hope that you will inform the state of Maine and the federal government about these loathsome grievances. I have physical evidence, which I spoke to you about, to corroborate this communiqué.

Sincerely,
James Richardson

Appendix C

Camden and Bowdoin, here is a record of all the child support I have paid and continue to pay to support you both. This is in additional to all the money Lucinda stole from me that the court determined past child support. This includes my $17,000 dismemberment check. I bet you never saw a penny of all this money.

3/10/08	$370.00
4/10/08	$370.00
5/14/08	$370.00
6/7/08	$370.00
7/8/08	$336.00
8/10/08	$30.00
9/7/08	$30.00
9/27/08	$87.38
10/4/08	$87.38
10/11/08	$87.38
10/18/08	$87.38
10/22/08	$87.38
10/29/08	$87.38

11/6/08	$87.38
11/13/08	$87.38
11/20/08	$87.38
11/26/08	$87.38
12/3/08	$87.38
12/10/08	$87.38
12/18/08	$87.38
12/24/08	$87.38
1/1/09	$87.38
1/6/09	$87.38
1/13/09	$87.38
1/17/09	$87.38
1/28/09	$87.38
2/4/09	$87.38
2/12/09	$87.38
2/19/09	$87.38
2/25/09	$87.38
3/3/09	$641.00 IRS Return
3/5/09	$87.38
3/12/09	$87.38
3/19/09	$87.38
3/26/09	$87.38
4/2/09	$87.38
4/9/09	$87.38
4/17/09	$87.38
4/22/09	$87.38
5/1/09	$87.38
5/7/09	$87.38
5/20/09	$87.38
5/23/09	$742.00 Social Security payment
5/27/09	$87.38
6/3/09	$742.00 Social Security payment
6/11/09	$87.38
6/17/09	$87.38
6/25/09	$87.38

7/2/09	$742.00 Social Security payment
7/3/09	$87.38
7/9/09	$250.00 S.S.I. American Recovery and Reinvestment Act
7/9/09	$87.38
7/16/09	$87.38
7/23/09	$87.38
7/28/09	$87.38
8/5/09	$87.38
8/5/09	$742.00 Social Security payment
8/12/09	$87.38
8/20/09	$87.38
8/27/09	$87.38
9/1/09	$87.38
9/3/09	$742.00 Social Security payment
9/9/09	$87.38
9/16/09	$87.38
9/23/09	$87.38
9/30/09	$87.38
10/2/09	$742.00 Social Security Payment
10/8/09	$87.38
10/14/09	$87.38
10/21/09	$87.38
10/28/09	$87.38
11/3/09	$742.00 Social Security Payment
11/4/09	$87.38
11/12/09	$87.38
11/19/09	$87.38
11/26/09	$87.38
12/2/09	$87.38
12/3/09	$742.00 Social Security Payment
12/9/09	$87.38
12/17/09	$87.38
12/23/09	$87.38
12/30/09	$87.38

1/4/10	$742.00 Social Security Payment
1/7/10	$50.19
1/13/10	$87.38
1/21/10	$61.28
1/28/10	$87.38
2/3/10	$81.57
2/3/10	$742.00 Social Security Payment
2/11/10	$87.38
2/19/10	$87.38
2/25/10	$87.38
3/2/10	$742.00 Social Security Payment

Appendix D

1/1/10

Dear Lucinda:

Now that the New Year is upon us I would like to think that we both can make some changes for the benefit of our sons. It has now been well over six years since my accident and well over five years since our divorce. We both know what happened .... And for my part, I promise to do the following things which should alleviate if not eliminate **most**, if not **all**, of your concerns regarding me and my relationship with my sons.

I will no longer reference anything in my correspondences to Camden and Bowdoin whether in writing (notes, cards etc.) or orally regarding my accident or what was said and/or done leading up to it or the events that occurred soon after it when I was convalescing in hospitals and the nursing home. I have become awakened figuratively and literally to the wisdom and power of Jesus Christ as my Lord and Savior. In brief, I now know it is not my place to judge the actions of others. "Vengeance is mine, says the Lord. I shall repay." I will no longer attempt to punish you for what occurred in 2003... In fact I wish you all the best for I now know that will positively affect my sons. I am sorry it took me so long to realize this.

Lucinda I want to become an integral part of my sons' lives. I hope and pray that you will no longer disparage me or my parents in front of Camden and Bowdoin. I can and will promise that I and my parents will not demean you in front of the boys. As you must be aware, this negatively impacts them. It hurt me and my mom when my mom asked Bowdoin to come into the house and he said "I can't, I am not allowed to." For this to work, the boys need to feel safe when they are with me. I could see from the window that Camden threw a fit in the back of Norm's car when he was asked to come out and go into my house to see me. Imagine for a minute how that made me feel let alone how that made Bowdoin and Camden feel. This must **end now** for the betterment of everyone involved especially Camden and Bowdoin. Will you please discontinue speaking ill of me or my family in front of the boys? Lucinda let us start anew in 2010.

A few months ago when you called one time you said "What do you want me to do? Kill myself." No Lucinda I don't want you to kill yourself. Our boys need **both** of us. I have missed so much of their lives ever since the accident. Lucinda I want to become an integral part of their lives. Will you please let me? Can we please pick a day and time of the week for the boys to call me or I can call them? We can, if you want, alter who calls whom every week. Let me know what you think of this. If for some reason either one of us can't make the time for the phone call, we could e-mail each other to inform the other one that something is coming up could we talk on such and such a date and time? Do you know what I mean? How does that sound?

Lucinda I am growing tired of throwing the divorce decree in your face and I am sure that you are increasingly weary hearing about it. When you really think about it, I am not asking too much. Please let me know what is going on in their lives and let me be part of that. Examples might include things that are going in their lives academically and/or socially at school or in athletic endeavors. It might be early now, but it won't be for long for them to be interested in girls and have girlfriends and I would like to know about that and be a part of it. Could you please send me some pictures of the boys in their athletic uniforms playing sports? That would mean a lot to me.

I am asking you to keep me informed as to the living situation of you and Camden and Bowdoin. If you remember correctly you kept Arthur informed of our living situation when we were together for his sake and Cassandra's. I am not asking for anything more, so will you please keep me abreast of this. According to my attorney and the divorce decree, I am entitled to this. I only have the best interests of my sons at heart. I would like to think and feel that if/when I send money or tickets down for the boys to come see me over summer vacation that you would actually allow them to come and spend time with their father. Will you?

Sincerely,
James

PS: Happy New Year Camden and Bowdoin